Essay Clinic

A Structural Guide to Essay Writing

CHARLES FLETCHER
Albury High School, NSW

M

Copyright © Charles Fletcher 1990

All rights reserved.
Except under the conditions described in the
Copyright Act 1968 of Australia and subsequent amendments,
no part of this publication may be reproduced,
stored in a retrieval system, or transmitted in any form or by any means,
electronic, mechanical, photocopying, recording or otherwise,
without the prior permission of the copyright owner.

First published 1990 by
MACMILLAN EDUCATION AUSTRALIA PTY LTD
107 Moray Street, South Melbourne 3205
6 Clarke Street, Crows Nest 2065
Reprinted 1991, 1993 (twice)

Associated companies and representatives
throughout the world

National Library of Australia
cataloguing in publication data

Fletcher, Charles.
　Essay clinic: a structural approach to essay writing.
　ISBN 0 7329 0201 0.
　1. Report writing. 2. English language – Rhetoric.
I. Title.

808.042

Typeset in Plantin by Graphicraft Typesetters Ltd., Hong Kong
Printed in Hong Kong

Illustrations by Tricia McCallum
Cover design by Jan Schmoeger

CONTENTS

Preface	vii
Acknowledgements	viii

1 Understanding the Question — 1
Why understanding is important — 1
Common directional terms — 2
Exercise 1: Analysing the question — 3

2 Planning — 4
Why planning works — 4
Planning stages — 6
Planning a descriptive essay — 7
Exercise 2: Planning — 8

3 Writing — 9
Why structure is vital — 9
Drafting — 10
Translating your plan into paragraphs — the introduction, the body paragraphs and the conclusion — 11
Exercise 3: Drafting an introduction — 14
Exercise 4: Drafting body paragraphs — 17
Exercise 5: Drafting the conclusion — 19
Putting it all together — 20
Exercise 6: Drafting an essay — 22
Descriptive essays for evaluation
   Topic set: 'Describe a ski resort' — 23

4 The Narrative Essay — 27
Exercise 7: Planning a narrative essay — 31
Exercise 8: Constructing a narrative essay — 31
Narrative essays for evaluation
   Topic set: 'Tell the story of your life' — 32

5 The Discursive Essay — 35
Exercise 9: Planning a discursive essay — 40
Exercise 10: Constructing a discursive essay — 40
Discursive essays for evaluation
   Topic set: 'Discuss the effects that television has had on us' — 42

6	**The Expository Essay**	46
	Exercise 11: Planning an expository essay	50
	Exercise 12: Constructing an expository essay	50
	Expository essays for evaluation	
	Topic set: 'Explain how to drive a manual car'	51
7	**The Analytical Essay**	56
	Exercise 13: Planning an analytical essay	60
	Exercise 14: Constructing an analytical essay	60
	Analytical essays for evaluation	
	Topic set: 'Analyse the role of the police in Australia'	61
8	**The Argumentative Essay**	65
	Exercise 15: Planning an argumentative essay	67
	Exercise 16: Constructing an argumentative essay	70
	Argumentative essays for evaluation	
	Topic set: 'Should capital punishment be re-introduced in Australia?'	70
9	**Common Faults in Written Expression**	75
	Avoiding errors	75
	Exercise 17: Avoiding colloquialisms and slang	76
	Exercise 18: Avoiding cliches	76
	Exercise 19: Avoiding tautology	77
	Exercise 20: Avoiding ambiguity	78
	Exercise 21: Using commas	78
	Exercise 22: Using apostrophes	78
	Exercise 23: Using quotation marks	79
	Exercise 24: Using the right tense	79
	Exercise 25: Avoiding muddled sentences	80
	Exercise 26: Avoiding long sentences	80
10	**Formal Essay Conventions**	82
	Synopsis	83
	Quotations	83
	Footnotes	84
	Bibliography	85

PREFACE

Many students find that the senior school makes heavy demands on their writing skills. As a senior student, you are expected to respond to abstract issues and concepts, often in a formal and structured way. It is the formal essay which is frequently used as a means of measuring your understanding of what you have studied.

While there is no substitute for a sound knowledge of your material, there are organisational skills associated with essay writing which you should recognise, acquire and practise.

The aim of this book is to give senior students a series of structural models on which to base their essays. The approach taken emphasises *method* above all else; no attempt is made to deal with the creative aspect of essay writing.

Students are encouraged to become careful planners who are prepared to think things through before they begin to write. This approach asks them to have faith in a method of question analysis, planning, paragraphing and editing. In return, students who master this method can expect to be able to produce an essay which is relevant to the question, organised in structure and has something useful to say to readers.

Students are helped to gain greater control of their written expression through elimination of basic errors.

ACKNOWLEDGEMENTS

The author is indebted to the following people for their assistance in the writing of this book:

Marge Files for her patience and her honest criticism; Ian Meikle for his help with sample essays and advice on Victorian schools' essay requirements; Anne Phair, Ken Perrin and Gary Cameron for their comments and practical advice; the English staff of Rutherglen High School for their courteous assistance with sample essays; Albury High School students from Years 10 and 11 who have kindly consented to the use of their essays in the 'essays for evaluation' sections; Mandy, my wife, for her honest criticism, her assistance with typing and her tolerance of the mess during the writing process.

CHAPTER 1
Understanding the Question

WHY UNDERSTANDING IS IMPORTANT

Think of an essay question as a set of instructions for a journey. The first task for the writer, as for the traveller, is to be clear about the instructions given. What direction has been specified? What territory must be crossed? If the writer has a clear understanding of the territory or topic on the one hand, and of the direction specified on the other, then he or she has the necessary information for planning an essay that will be *relevant* to the question.

The steps you are about to follow in the next two chapters concern the preparations to be made before any writing is done.

• ANALYSE THE QUESTION

You determine what is relevant when you analyse your question. This involves taking the question apart so that its components, and then the whole, can be understood. There are two essential parts to a question: one is the *direction* part and the other is the *topic* part.

Steps of analysis:

1. Read the question carefully, several times.

2. (Circle) the *directional* words.

3. Underline the main *topic* words.

Examples:

(a) From your reading of his cases, (describe) Sherlock Holmes.

(b) (What happened) to the Tasmanian Aborigines?

(c) (Who) is the most important character in 'Lord of the Flies' and (how much) has he changed by the end of the novel?

(d) Capital punishment should be re-introduced. (Do you agree?)

COMMON DIRECTIONAL TERMS

Here are some common directional terms that you will need to know:

Outline	Give the main points, usually in a sensible order.
Account for	Offer an explanation of how/why something happened.
How	Offer an explanation of/for something.
Why	Give the reasons for something.
Explain	Give a clear account of what happened and offer reasons for it happening.
Discuss	Give points for and against, based on evidence, and draw a conclusion from points presented.

Compare	Point out similarities based on evidence. (Some contrast may also need to be made.)
Contrast	Stress differences based on evidence. (Some comparison may also need to be made.)
State	Present clearly and concisely.
Comment on	Express a personal opinion based on evidence.
To what extent/ How far do you agree	Quantify your agreement/disagreement with a given statement.

Exercise 1: Analysing the question

Using the underline and circle system, analyse the following questions:

(1) Outline the main problems that face Australia's biggest cities.
(2) Australia should have a new flag. Comment on this suggestion.
(3) Describe the journey undertaken by the First Fleet.
(4) Discuss the claim that alcohol presents our greatest drug problem.
(5) Compare television news services with those offered by newspapers. What are the advantages and disadvantages of each?

Now review your analysis of each question:

CHECKLIST
- Do I understand all terms used?
- Have I isolated all directional terms?
- Have main topic terms now been made clear?
- In questions with more than one part, have I noted the directions and topics relevant to each part?

Where a question has more than one part, try allocating marks to each part. This method will help you to avoid spending too much time on one part of a question at the expense of another part. Remember that the marker of the essay will be using a similar method of allocation. In the case of a 'how and why' question, for instance, you could expect to allocate half the possible marks and about half the time to each part.

Question analysis is a vital step in the preparation of an essay. Now you have a system which can be applied to all questions. Use the system and be confident that you have done the groundwork.

CHAPTER 2
Planning

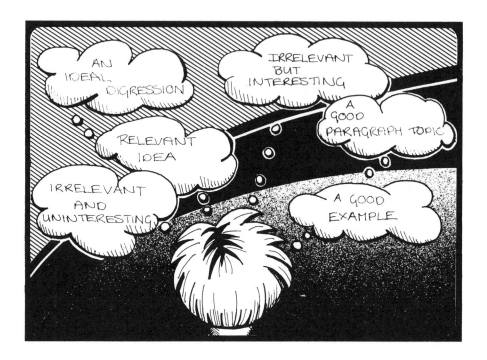

WHY PLANNING WORKS

> A plan is a blueprint for the shape, order and direction of an essay.

The great advantage of a sound plan is that it enables you to see what your essay will look like before you start writing.

Planning will help you to use your time more efficiently. Once you are used to planning, you will find essay writing a smoother process because you will have 'ironed out' problems and set your course at the planning stage.

A plan should be prepared for every essay you write. This applies both to research essays written over a week and to those written in class.

Each plan should be in *point-form*. It should be a 'skeleton' of brief points, which allows you to see the shape the essay will take. With a point-form plan you will be able to:
- list points for possible inclusion
- decide the relevance of each point
- decide the *status* of each point (i.e. as a paragraph topic or as an example)
- match points with appropriate examples
- check the plan against the terms of the question
- make changes quickly and easily
- give each paragraph a job to do.

It is of paramount importance that you understand the link between points in a plan and paragraphs in an essay. Each main point in a plan is expanded into a paragraph dealing with that particular idea.

Example 1

(Describe) Count Dracula.

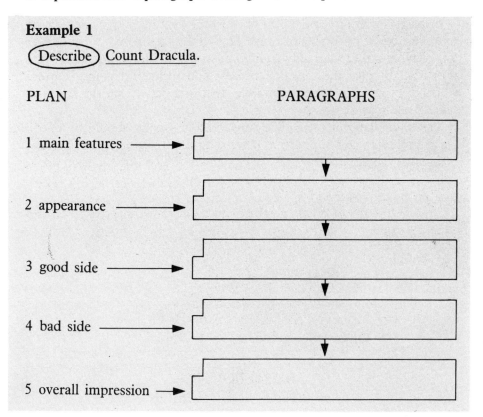

Note that the topic of each paragraph is never in doubt after the planning is completed. Much of the hard work has been done before the writing phase begins.

PLANNING STAGES

The planning stages you use once you have analysed the question are very important because they ensure the relevance of your essay and the order of its material. Each planning stage should be seen as a *careful-thinking operation*, and *the value of these operations should be reflected in the time that you allow for them*. Read each of the following operations as a thinking task rather than as a writing task.

> - ANALYSE THE QUESTION

>> - SELECT RELEVANT POINTS
>> - DECIDE STATUS OF POINTS

Instead of waiting for the best or most relevant ideas to come floating into your head, try brainstorming. This first step involves turning over lots of ideas rather than only trying to come up with the best ones. It is important to start the selection process and to keep it going. Do not worry if a few ideas have to be discarded; it is better that the selection takes place now rather than later.

The second step involves deciding whether a point should become a paragraph topic or a supporting point within a paragraph. One method of isolating paragraph topics is to box them. When this has been done, arrows may be used to link the relevant supporting points to the appropriate paragraph topic.

Once the status of points has been decided, they can be ordered and expanded upon.

> - ANALYSE THE QUESTION

>> - SELECT RELEVANT POINTS
>> - DECIDE STATUS OF POINTS

>>> - ORDER POINTS
>>> - MAKE SUBDIVISIONS

PLANNING A DESCRIPTIVE ESSAY

> A descriptive essay presents an organised word picture. It should make an impact on the reader's senses.

Descriptive essays may appear to rely on creativity rather than on planning for their impact, but the principle of careful planning is still needed if an essay is to be relevant and clear in its description.

Look at the following example of a descriptive essay plan. What particular organisational tasks are evident in this plan?

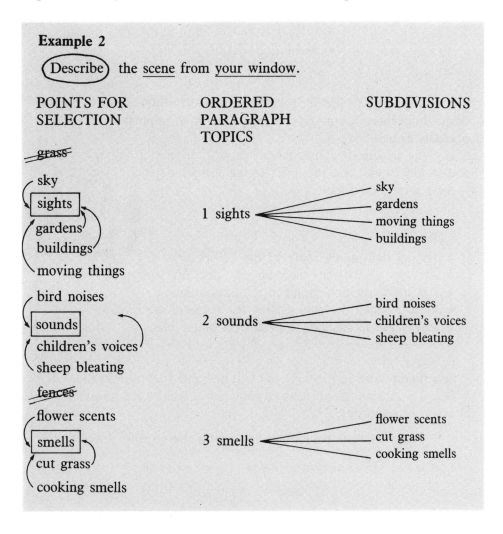

Exercise 2: Planning
Prepare a plan for each of the following descriptive essay questions:
(1) Describe a beach scene.
(2) Describe Santa Claus.
  In planning for each essay, use the method demonstrated to:

- ANALYSE THE QUESTION

- SELECT RELEVANT POINTS
- DECIDE STATUS OF POINTS

- ORDER POINTS
- MAKE SUBDIVISIONS

You may refer to previous examples and definitions as often as you wish. Be prepared to make changes. This is an important part of the planning process.

Use the headings 'points for selection', 'ordered paragraph topics' and 'subdivisions' as a reminder of the planning stages.

Now review each plan:

---CHECKLIST---
- Have I thoroughly analysed the question?
- Are my subdivisions more specific than my paragraph topics?
- Are my paragraph topics in a logical order?
- Have I tested the plan against the terms of the question?
- Have I made changes to produce a better plan?

When you write your essay, you will be guided by the 'skeleton' that you make in your plan. Always plan before you write, even for the simplest of questions.

** Keep each of your plans for use in the writing phase **

CHAPTER 3
Writing

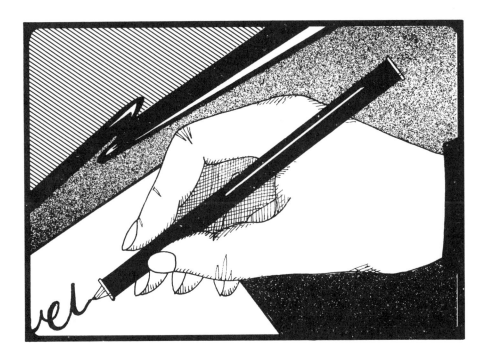

WHY STRUCTURE IS VITAL

Before you begin writing your essay, you should be prepared to:

Write for a particular audience
All writers have an obligation to see that what they write is appropriate for their intended audience. School essays are mostly written for an *informed* audience. An informed audience will know the material and will be more interested in your comments, observations and interpretations rather than in your ability to re-tell stories or summarise events.

Write to a plan

Once you are satisfied that your plan provides a sound framework for your written response to a question, you must follow that plan. Although it may seem awkward at first, writing to a plan makes the writing task easier because there are clear steps to follow. It is also safer, because you can test the relevance of your answer before you begin to write the essay.

Draft your written response

During the writing phase of essay construction, your plan is translated into paragraphs. Read the following section on drafting and decide for yourself the importance of the drafting process.

DRAFTING

> A draft is a particular version of a piece of writing. Drafting is the process of writing and then re-writing. This process of making changes ensures that the writer's intended meaning is conveyed more clearly and simply.

When you write an essay under test conditions, you are unlikely to have the time to do more than one draft. This makes the plan all the more critical. However, when you are allowed several days to write an essay, it will be expected that your finished product will have been carefully drafted.

The drafted paragraph below is an introduction to a descriptive essay answering the question 'Describe Count Dracula'. Look carefully at the changes that have been made to the original draft.

Example 3

FIRST DRAFT

~~Count Dracula was an expert at concealing the truth.~~ ↓
~~He~~ impressed people with his ~~manners~~ *sophistication* and his apparent good will towards ~~his victims~~ *everyone*. He fooled the victims with this good side *of his nature*. ~~and they realised this too late.~~
He was driven to ~~kill~~ *action* by the dark side of his character, which dominated him.

SECOND DRAFT

Count Dracula impressed people with his ~~sophistication~~ sophisticated appearance, and ~~his apparent good will towards everyone. He fooled the victims~~ with ~~this~~ the good side of his nature, ~~and~~ he won their trust. ~~He was driven to action by~~ The dark side of his character, ~~which~~ drove him to action and dominated him.

THIRD DRAFT

Count Dracula impressed people with his ~~sophisticated~~ appearance, and with the good side of his nature ~~he~~. However, it was the (won their trust) ~~The~~ bad side ~~of~~ his character that dominated and drove him to action ~~and dominated him~~.

FINAL DRAFT

Count Dracula impressed people with his appearance, and won their trust with the good side of his nature. However, it was the bad side that dominated his character and drove him to action.

Find examples of the following changes:
- to insert
- to delete (i.e. take out)
- to re-order
- to clarify

Paragraphs that will probably require the most drafting are the *introduction* and *conclusion*.

TRANSLATING YOUR PLAN INTO PARAGRAPHS

There are three types of paragraph that you must be able to use in formal essays. Each of these has a specific function in terms of the type of information that it presents to the reader.

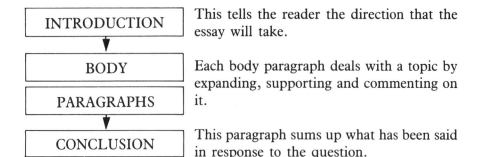

INTRODUCTION	This tells the reader the direction that the essay will take.
BODY PARAGRAPHS	Each body paragraph deals with a topic by expanding, supporting and commenting on it.
CONCLUSION	This paragraph sums up what has been said in response to the question.

Each type of paragraph will be examined in detail in the following pages. As you read each section, ask yourself how important the plan has become by this stage, and whether a well-prepared plan makes the writing task easier.

The plans that you prepared in exercise 2 will be required during this section, beginning with plan (1). This will be your chance to see how your careful thinking in the planning phase will pay off when it comes to constructing the paragraphs.

The Introduction

• SET DIRECTIONS

An introduction is your first contact with the reader. It should tell the reader where you are about to take him or her, just as a signpost directs travellers.

An introduction should:
- capture the reader's attention
- warn the reader of the main points to be made in later paragraphs (i.e. paragraph topics)
- warn the reader of the particular approach adopted towards the subject of the essay
- set a clear direction in response to the terms of the question
- end when the job is done.

An introduction should not:
- ramble
- start a discussion (body paragraphs will do this where necessary)
- ignore the terms of the question
- mention specific examples or state facts
- confuse the reader.

Example 4

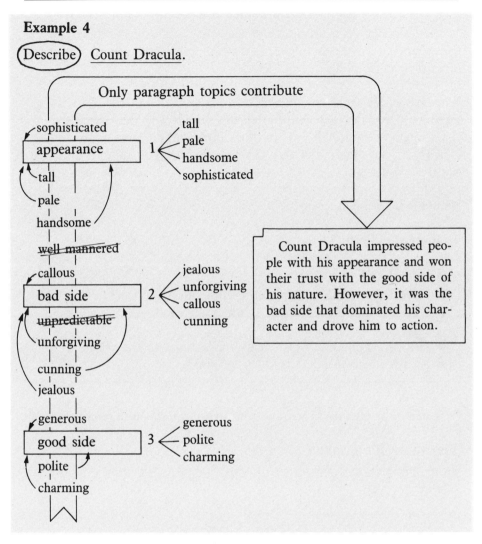

Has this introduction *set a clear direction* for the reader to follow? Have you been warned what to expect in the body paragraphs? Read the paragraph through carefully. Have specific details been included? Check the plan for differences between paragraph topics and subdivisions. Look, for instance, at the difference between 'appearance' and 'tall'. Only paragraph topics should have contributed to this introduction; the subdivisions or specific details, 'tall', 'jealous' and so on, must be left for the body paragraphs.

With so much important information to be transmitted through the introduction, you can understand why *clarity of expression* is essential. Never be afraid to use short sentences to ensure that your intention is clear. You want your reader to follow you into the body paragraphs.

The length of each introduction may vary according to the length of the essay, but as a general rule, four to six lines should be sufficient for most essays.

Exercise 3: Drafting an introduction
Examine the plans that you drafted in exercise 2. Take special note of the paragraph topics. Now, draft an introduction from plan number (1). Take your time; this is a *method* exercise. You may do as many drafts as you wish.

Remember: Set Directions

Now review your introduction:

---CHECKLIST---
- Have I given the reader a clear direction to follow?
- Have I warned the reader of the main subdivisions within my essay?
- Has my expression been clear, concise and to the point?
- As a reader, do I feel ready to go on?

** Keep your plan and introduction together for use in exercise 4. **

The Body Paragraphs

- SET DIRECTIONS

- EXPAND
- SUPPORT
- LINK

Each body paragraph is based on a topic prepared for in your plan. It must also fit into the essay's sequence of paragraphs by making links with the question and with other paragraphs.

A body paragraph should:
- expand on its topic using the minor subdivisions
- support its topic with specific details and/or examples
- make links with the question and with other paragraphs.

A body paragraph should not:
- ramble
- stray from its planned topic
- ignore the directional terms of the question
- deal with material outside the terms of the question, no matter how interesting it may be.

When beginning a paragraph, your first step is to write the *topic sentence*. The topic sentence tells the reader what the paragraph will be about. It is usually the first sentence in a paragraph. The topic sentence is underlined in example 5.

Example 5
Match this with example 4.

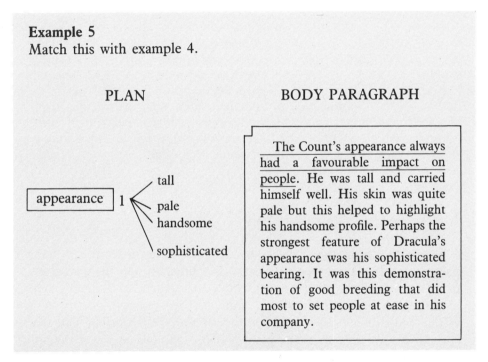

The topic sentence in a body paragraph is simple to construct. All the writer has to do is to take the paragraph topic from the plan and convert this to a sentence. This topic sentence should be worded in fairly general terms because it serves as an introduction to the paragraph. Does the above example illustrate this? Look at the difference between 'favourable' and 'handsome', for instance.

Now study the remainder of the paragraph. Does it keep strong links with the plan? Are points in the plan treated in the same order in the paragraph? What sort of job does the final sentence do for this paragraph? Discuss your responses to these questions with other students.

Example 6
Match this with example 2.

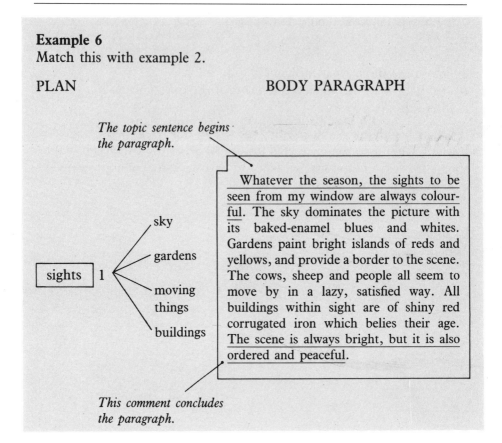

The points from the plan are used in the same order in the body paragraph. The topic sentence sets the direction for the paragraph using comparatively general terms. (Note that 'colourful' is more general than 'baked-enamel blues' and 'shiny red'.)

The bulk of a body paragraph should be spent dealing with the specific details set out in the plan, but the *intention* of the paragraph should never be forgotten. It is the topic sentence that reminds the writer of this intention.

The final sentence of the paragraph in example 6 is different from the preceding sentences. It sums up what the paragraph has said and *links* the paragraph with the question by way of a concluding comment. Each body paragraph's comment will be important when it is time to write the conclusion of the essay.

Now read both paragraphs again. Have the topics been *expanded*? Have they been *supported* with specific examples? Finally, have the paragraphs been *linked* to the question? Find evidence to support your response in each case.

Exercise 4: Drafting body paragraphs

For this exercise you will need your plan and introduction from exercise 3. Re-read each of them before you begin.

Your task here is to expand your plan into body paragraphs. Most of the hard work has already been done in the plan. Feel free to go back to any definitions or examples that may be of use.

Remember: Expand; Support; Link.

Now review your body paragraphs:

---CHECKLIST---
- Is the topic of each paragraph made clear at the outset?
- Have all the subdivisions of the plan been translated into the text of the paragraphs?
- Has my final sentence in each paragraph rounded off the paragraph?

** Keep your plan, introduction and body paragraphs together **
for use in exercise 5.

The Conclusion

- SET DIRECTIONS

- EXPAND
- SUPPORT
- LINK

- TIE TOGETHER
- SUM UP
- MAKE JUDGEMENTS

The conclusion is even more important than the introduction as it draws together the threads of the essay to arrive at some useful outcome or judgement. This summing up must respond directly to the terms of the question. To do this, you, the writer, must weigh up and tie together the concluding comments of each paragraph. Remember, your concluding paragraph must satisfy the reader that you have understood, thought about, and fully answered the question.

A conclusion should:
- tie together comments made earlier in the text of the essay
- sum up what has been said in response to the terms of the question, particularly where more than one point of view is involved
- make judgements that carry some weight and that are within the terms of the question
- show some insight into the topic written about.

A conclusion should not:
- be a re-worded introduction
- continue a discussion
- bring in new material or supporting evidence. (This is not to say that we should rule out the suggestion of new alternatives or hint at new directions in a conclusion. Conclusions should allow such suggestions as long as these are consistent with the preceding text.)

You will find most of the material for the conclusion in the comments that you have made in the body of the essay. If you find conclusions difficult to write, it may be that you have not been commenting on points made in the body paragraphs.

Perhaps one of the most satisfying characteristics of a good conclusion is that it reflects an original way of looking at things. It is this original response to a question which shows the reader that the writer has been prepared to think things through.

Example 7
Match this with examples 4 and 5.

This statement briefly summarises what the essay has shown.

This statement is a general observation that can now be made.

The final sentence gives the reader a verdict or decision that is consistent with the question.

CONCLUSION

Dracula was certainly a strange figure. He represented the best and worst in man, but these extremes were not in balance. His goodness was only skin-deep, while his heart was black and cold. Dracula, the man, was only a shell covering the fiend within.

Look back at the introductory paragraph in example 4. How is the introduction different from the conclusion? Are the two paragraphs interchangeable? How important are the points made in the conclusion? Do these points leave the reader satisfied that the question has been answered? Think about these questions as you follow example 8.

Example 8
Match this with examples 2 and 6.

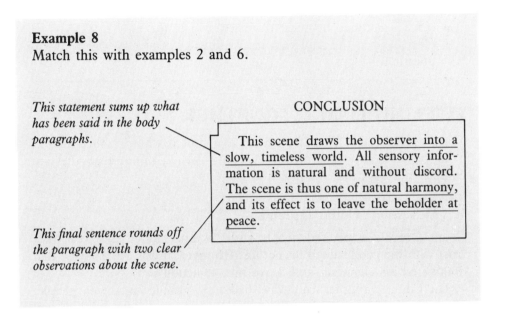

What things are said here that would not be appropriate in the introduction? Does this conclusion *tie together* the main threads explored earlier in examples 2 and 6? (For instance, are sights, sounds and smells drawn together by one comment?) Does it *sum up* what has been shown? Finally, has the writer been able to answer the question? For instance, what sort of scene is it, and what has been the effect on the observer?

Exercise 5: Drafting the conclusion
For this exercise, you will need the plan, introduction and body paragraphs from exercise 4. Re-read all of your paragraphs before you begin.
   Your task is to draft the conclusion, the most important paragraph of the essay.

Remember: Tie together; Sum up; Make judgements

Now review your conclusion:

> **CHECKLIST**
> - Have I tied together comments made in the body paragraphs?
> - Where necessary, have I weighed alternative views against each other?
> - Have I summed up what has been said in the essay?
> - Have I given the reader an interesting and useful answer to the question?

PUTTING IT ALL TOGETHER

You should be able to read an essay as a united whole, rather than as a jumble of component pieces. Keeping this in mind, read the two completed essays that follow.

1. (Describe) Count Dracula.

Count Dracula impressed people with his appearance and won their trust with the good side of his nature. However, it was the bad side that dominated his character and drove him to action.

The Count's appearance always had a favourable impact on people. He was tall and carried himself well. His skin was quite pale but this helped to highlight his handsome profile. Perhaps the strongest feature of Dracula's appearance was his sophisticated bearing. It was this air of good breeding that did most to set people at ease in his company.

Most observers saw Dracula as a good-natured man. He was unfailingly polite when introduced to people and he gave the impression that he was a socialite whose role in life was to give pleasure to others. Ladies always found him to be a charming host; men felt that their wives and daughters were safe in his hands. Dracula showed his support for charities, particularly for the Red Cross Blood Bank. Here, it seemed, was one of the true gentlemen of Europe.

Survivors told of the darker side of the man's nature. While he charmed the women, he was insanely jealous of competition and frequently murdered young men who posed a threat to his influence. Those who were critical or disloyal were eventually lured to ghastly fates. This cruel and cunning mind was the last thing people expected of Dracula, but his victims soon discovered that it was only a veneer of civilisation which covered Europe's greatest monster.

Dracula was certainly a strange figure; he represented the best and the worst in man, but these extremes were not in balance. His goodness was only skin-deep, while his heart was black and cold. Count Dracula, the man, was but a shell covering the fiend within.

2. (Describe) the scene from your window.

There is much to sense from my window. The sights are colourful, the sounds are soothing and the smells are intoxicating. Throughout the year, the scene is pleasantly peaceful for all who are fortunate enough to be part of it.

Whatever the season, the sights to be seen from my window are always colourful. The sky dominates the picture with its baked-enamel blues and whites. Gardens paint bright islands of reds and yellows, and provide a border to the scene. The cows, sheep and people all seem to move by in a lazy, satisfied way. All buildings within sight are of shiny red corrugated iron which belies their age. The scene is always bright, ordered and peaceful.

All sounds reaching my room have a soothing effect on the listener. The finches, wrens and magpies are there to wake the household with their exuberant morning calls. Children's voices come floating across from the swings in the pine trees, their giggles rippling out over the paddocks. Sheep bleat contentedly in the background or call lazily to their lambs. These sounds reflect a slow pace of life in a natural environment.

A subtle but intoxicating range of scents is the most powerful aspect of the scene. Rose perfumes drift through the house and cure any staleness lingering there. Outside, the scent of cut grass sweetly recommends itself to all. Fresh and steamy apricot pies or roasts waft their flavours around the garden during the long summer days. The strength of these fragrances comes not from richness but from a soft, drug-like effect which makes everyone forget the passing of time.

This scene draws the observer into a slow, timeless world. All sensory information is natural and without discord. The scene is thus one of natural harmony, and its effect is to leave the beholder at peace.

* * *

Is each essay a united whole? If it has been written in clear steps, the essay should not only be easy to follow, but it should also allow the reader to construct a plan from the essay paragraphs. Is this possible for each of these essays?

Look closely at the paragraphs. Are you able to identify links with the plan? Is each paragraph performing its task as an introduction, body paragraph or conclusion? How can you tell? Are you able to identify different levels of detail chosen for the various paragraphs?

Most importantly, you must ask yourself if you are satisfied that each essay has answered the question.

Now put yourself in the reader's position and carefully read over the descriptive essay you completed in exercise 5 ('Describe a beach scene'). Is it possible to construct a plan from the paragraphs? Is the essay a united whole? Ask other readers for their opinions and for any constructive criticisms they may have to offer.

Exercise 6: Drafting an essay

The essay that you have completed came from a plan drafted in exercise 2. One other plan was also drafted there, for the question 'Describe Santa Claus'. Draft an essay response to this question according to the steps you have been shown. Remember:

- ANALYSE THE QUESTION

- SELECT RELEVANT POINTS
- DECIDE STATUS OF POINTS

- ORDER POINTS
- MAKE SUBDIVISIONS

- SET DIRECTIONS

- EXPAND
- SUPPORT
- LINK

- TIE TOGETHER
- SUM UP
- MAKE JUDGEMENTS

Now review your essay:

CHECKLIST
- Have I made clear what I am describing?
- Have I planned for a particular angle of approach (e.g. sights, sounds, smells, rather than still things, slow things, fast things)?
- Have I been consistent in following this planned approach?
- Have I written a description rather than a narrative?
- Have I given the reader a 'weak' ending or one that makes an impact?

Additional descriptive Essay Questions
(1) Describe a frosty morning in the country.
(2) Describe Paul Hogan.
(3) Describe Australia to someone who has no knowledge of it.

About This Section

This is the first of six sections containing essays written by students from Years 10 and 11. The other sections deal with *narrative, discursive, expository, analytical* and *argumentative* modes of essay.

The intention of each of the 'essays for evaluation' sections is to give you a range of responses to the same question. Within this range there will be certain strengths and weaknesses which you should be able to recognise and comment on.

As you read each set of samples, see if you can place the essays in order of merit, taking into account: whether the response is relevant to the question; whether each response is logically organised; and whether the paragraphs in each essay have done their job.

Specifically, you might ask:

- Is the writer's intention clear?
- What angle of approach has been taken?

- Is this approach consistent throughout?
- Can you see any contradictions that weaken the structure of the essay?
- Are the examples relevant?
- Is there continuity between paragraphs?
- Does the conclusion draw the threads of the essay together?
- Is the essay a united whole?

Try making your own point-form notes on each essay under the headings 'strengths' and 'weaknesses'.

Compare your impressions of these essays with those of other readers. Do they see the same strengths and weaknesses? Do they disagree with your choice of the better essays?

> The *descriptive* essay question set for each of the three essays was: 'Describe a ski resort'.

Descriptive Essay A

The Yuppie Valley Resort is nestled into a natural hollow in the spine of a vast range. It stretches from the skyline to the valley floor. Skiers give or take away its life. By day the place is alive in every nerve; by night it is muted and still as nature reclaims her own.

At first light each building carries a heavy cloak on its shoulders, and waits stoically for spring. From the lodge and hotel windows, hundreds of expectant faces mime the same expression. In the sheds the packing machines doze, their paws and noses protruding. Beyond them, the chairlift cables haul the craggy peaks closer to the valley. From the mountain tops the Leggo town seems complete.

The mountain prepares for the inevitable onslaught. Early tourists stumble from buses onto the snow with strange, laboured steps. Seasoned veterans skate gracefully past them in co-ordinated colours. On the wider slopes, women sit down before they fall down. Wild men in football jerseys and beanies knock everyone down before being sent off. Austrian instructors survey the scene and sum up the madness with a shaking of heads.

A clear day brings the lodge-bunnies screaming, falling and slithering across the hillsides. There is no nook or cranny into which they will not fall. Nature seems to call them into every clump of trees. The mountain bears the insanity until the late afternoon, when it claims a few victims. As the sun fades, the great retreat begins.

The spidery hand of evening walks its fingers over the range and into the village, silencing the excesses of the day. Pedestrians' voices are subdued. Soon, the valley herds its guests into their burrows and order is restored. The scene settles to a winking painting, and night draws its curtain down.

This popular resort is a place of contrasts, both in the physical environment and in terms of human activity. A small settlement draws huge crowds of madmen to a fast-lane sport, yet the same place is a virtual nativity scene after dark. Despite its dramatic mood swings, the valley is on everyone's list for next year.

Descriptive Essay B

If you drive to the top of a mountain in North-East Victoria during winter, you will find a temporary piece of Europe perching on the summit. The people, buildings and the lifestyle are foreign to what we usually see in Australian resorts.

The mountain is rugged and steep. Snow covers its peak for four months of the year. Only a few areas on the summit have been developed — most is still untouched. This gives the skiers the opportunity to ski in a more natural setting, and sightseers are able to avoid the resort completely.

The resort has been well planned. All buildings are distinctly European in style with sloping roofs and no verandahs. There are no high-rise monsters here, buildings are timber and brick.

Apart from several glorious lodges, there are many restaurants and shops — also designed to suit the climate. The restaurants are warm and cosy, and smell delicious when you enter. The shops are quaint with friendly assistants to help you choose a souvenir or the right length of ski.

The lifts and tows up the slopes are well placed to prevent excessive scarring to the overall picture of the resort. The slopes themselves are basically unaltered — left as they were found when the resort began.

The people you find in this resort range from city sightseers to European ski instructors who travel the world to ski all year. There are families who travel up to see and experience the snow. Then there are the people brave enough to attempt skiing. After that — the people keen enough and rich enough to be able to ski each year are able to become quite experienced. There are people of all ages and cultures in the resort. The resort appeals to all people.

The ski resort is very popular as it gives Australians a taste of Europe, and Europeans feel comfortable in an environment close to their own. Above all, though, is the fact that the resort is beautiful. It lies in perfect harmony with the picturesque landscape of the mountain.

Descriptive Essay C

The Mount Terabula Ski Resort lies in a very idyllic setting, nestled in a valley. The tree-covered valley slopes down to form the snowfields, which are dotted with tiny human figures.

The resort, though artificial, lies in a perfectly natural setting. The surrounding mountains, tall and majestic, are covered with short stunted trees which are draped in snow. The mountains form a valley which creates the ski slopes the vacationers come for.

The white strips that are the skiing fields are covered with a thick carpet of snow, occasionally flecked with thick clumps of trees. Lifts decorate the scene, winding up the sides of the mountains. The slopes are also peppered with snow-loving holidaymakers.

There is a great variety of people on the slopes, from the professional skier to the novice tobogganer. Most are attired in thick, padded, warm clothing, and all are attempting to enjoy their various sports. There is a continual flow of the eager from the resort to the slopes, and an equal flow of the tired or injured into the warm resort.

The cluster of buildings that represents the resort of Terabula stands prominent. The lodge stands tall, capable of accommodating hundreds, while the office-block restaurant complex spreads across the grounds beside a variety of shops and a carpark. A trail of private and very expensive units lies to the rear of the administration building.

Therefore, when the resort of Terabula is in such beautiful surroundings, has adequate facilities and satisfied visitors, it is indeed an idyllic setting.

CHAPTER 4
The Narrative Essay

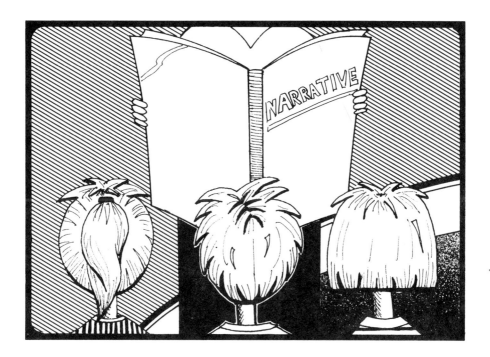

> A narrative essay tells a story.

Think about the difference between a description and a narration. A description paints a word-picture while a narrative advances the action. The descriptive essay on Dracula paints the different sides of his nature, but an essay that sets out to tell us about his life would be a narrative. A narrative essay does not merely give the reader information; it must have a story to tell, and it must hold the reader's interest until the end.

Generally speaking, a chronological approach is the safest way to plan a narrative essay. Imagine that you have been asked to give a narrative account of your life. A simple and logical way to plan your response would be to begin with infancy or early childhood, and then take each subsequent stage of life as it occurred in time. A chronological narrative is not your only option, but it is a simple way to structure this type of essay.

Examine the following plan of a narrative essay. Note the ways in which it is different from the descriptive form.

Example 9

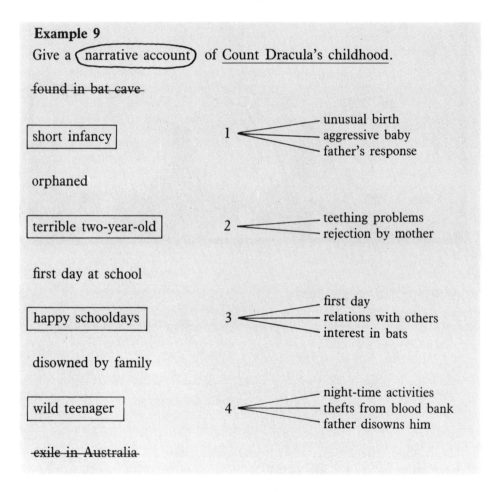

This plan divides Dracula's life into stages and deals mainly with his actions and the reactions of others. The narrative is presented through a series of events. Now examine the way this plan is developed into paragraphs.

THE NARRATIVE ESSAY

Give a (narrative account) of Count Dracula's Childhood.

Only paragraph topics contribute to the introduction.

A. Vlad Dracula sped through infancy to become a truly terrible two-year-old. His school days were generally happy, but he became a wild teenager and dashed the hopes his parents had held for him.

short infancy
- unusual birth
- aggressive baby
- father's response

The young Transylvanian had a very short infancy. His birth caused a stir in medical circles because of his physical maturity. He worried his mother with his aggression and he lost the sympathy of nurses whose blood he had begun to sample. Consequently, he was removed from hospital to the quiet exile of his father's castle. Here he was informed that his infancy was over.

terrible two-year-old
- teething problems
- rejection by mother

B. Vlad began a reign of terror as a two-year-old. His nightly teething troubles caused him to howl with a mournful animal cry; and during daylight hours he would attack the ankles of the slower castle servants. His mother began to distance herself from her suprisingly independent offspring. Soon, the bond which held mother and son together was broken, and she refused any further maternal role. In this sense, Dracula's own mother was his first casualty.

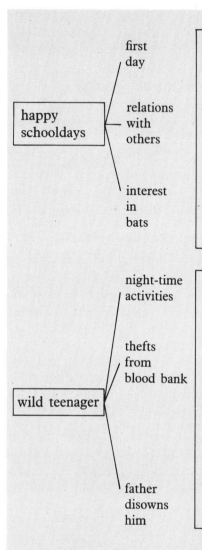

Schooldays were a happy time for the boy who was unhappy at home. He was impressed, on his first day, with the innocence of the other students. He liked the way in which so many potential victims were kept in one place. As the days passed, the other students gave him a cool reception, respecting those flashing incisors. His happiest hours were those spent in nature study with his relatives, the bats. <u>Despite his comparative isolation from other students, school was a place of great interest to Vlad, and he pleased his father with his academic success.</u>

C

The Dracula family could not have prepared itself for Vlad's wild teenage years. He lived for the night-time and shunned the rest of his family. News of Vlad's activities reached his father's ears. There were sightings of mysterious bats and wolves in the neighbourhood, and the blood bank in the village had been plundered repeatedly, despite tight security. Worst of all, Vlad would not account for his absences. He raged at his father when confronted with the evidence, and, each time, the father's faith in the boy ebbed away. With Vlad behaving more like a cornered animal than an aristocrat, his father formally disowned him, and Vlad's exile from the family was complete.

<u>Childhood for Dracula proved to be an experience both hurtful and rewarding.</u> It was a time of frustration and rejection but also one of discovery. The great passions of his childhood were also to be the passions of his later life. <u>Awkward relationships with his peers and his exile from the family circle foreshadowed the lonely life he would lead as an adult.</u> Though despised and misunderstood by many, Vlad Dracula knew, even as a child, that he would make his mark on the world.

D

E

Exercise 7: Planning a narrative essay

Re-read the narrative account of Dracula's childhood, keeping in mind the role each paragraph is performing. Now take each underlined extract, A to E, and decide:

(1) what it does in the paragraph
(2) what it does in the essay as a whole.

This narrative essay was planned according to the same steps that you used in your descriptive essays, and that you will be using with other types of essays later. You should now have a clearer understanding of the way in which a sound plan protects the structure of the whole essay.

Exercise 8: Constructing a narrative essay

Your task is to construct your own narrative essay based on the question: 'Give a narrative account of your life'.

Take your time; this is a method exercise. You have a clear set of steps to follow, and you should know the importance of a carefully drafted plan.

---CHECKLIST---
- Have I ordered my points chronologically?
- Do my paragraphs advance the action rather than paint a picture?
- Have I told a story that is clear and logical in its presentation?
- Is my essay a united whole?

A long narrative will not necessarily be a good one. Here are a few hints that may help you to keep your reader interested:
- Draft in order to improve clarity and simplicity.
- Include only things relevant to the progress of the narrative.
- Vary paragraph openings.
- Vary the length of your sentences.
- Avoid long-winded sentences.

Additional Narrative Essay Questions

(1) Give a narrative account of the life of a bunyip.
(2) What happened to the Tasmanian Aborigines?
(3) Tell the story of Australia's settlement from prehistoric times to the present day.

Narrative Essays for Evaluation

The *narrative* essay question set for each of the three essays was: 'Tell the story of your life'.

Narrative Essay A

My life began with an awkward birth. During infancy came the tasks of learning to walk and talk. I showed interest in surroundings at an early age. I started school at an early age and, being average academically, found it enjoyable. Adolescence was trying but filled with happy events.

I came into the world prematurely, by a Caesarian birth. There were difficulties, particularly with breathing, and allergic reactions to penicillin and to mother's milk. These first few days of my life were crucial. Most of the foods I ate then were determined by whether I reacted badly to them or not.

During infancy I was sick and caught pneumonia, German measles, mumps and chicken pox, but I did not get any major illnesses. I began to walk and talk early and began to show interest in my surroundings, and was always occupied. As a result, I was sent to school at the age of four.

School was a lot of fun and quite enjoyable despite my average academic success. At the age of nine I changed schools and gradually settled in to my new surroundings. High school was a little frightening at first, but I soon got used to its size and the different atmosphere.

Adolescence is my most memorable stage because it is the most recent. The beginning did not happen noticeably. It was the time that I began to develop a personality of my own, and stopped being influenced by others. Because I am smaller in size than most people, I found adolescence difficult, with people not recognising or believing my age.

Adolescence was also the time when I developed many interests such as horse riding, skating, dancing and music. Some of these I still continue; others I have left behind. During this time, which was trying for my parents and other members of my family, I gained my own beliefs and opinions. Only a few incidents in my life stand out. These include places I have been, such as Melbourne, Ballarat and Bendigo, and people I have met, such as Bob Hawke. Other things, such as moving house and meeting relatives from England that I never knew I had, have made life enjoyable in general.

I have learned in the past few years to accept myself as I am. My friends and other people around me seem to have done the same, preferring my friendship to material things. I believe that experiencing a wide range of hobbies and interests has helped me to establish my likes and dislikes and to become the person that I am.

Narrative Essay B

My life has been quite easy, especially during my late teen years in the country. I have a good group of friends and we enjoy each other's company, even though there are some strong differences between us.

When I was seven, I fell out of Dad's car as we went round a corner. Dad had forgotten to close the door. Everyone laughed about it later, but I can still remember the wheels of trucks humming past my nose as I lay on the tar. Soon after this, we moved out to the country and Dad left the Tactical Response Group in Sydney for a quiet life as an explosives expert in Walla. By the time I was ten, I was a proper country kid.

Mother had a surprise when I was born because she thought she was expecting twins. The whole family was waiting around with two sets of everything. I was not very popular there for a while. Apparently I slept well and did not annoy people as I do now. When I was four, my father left me at school by mistake. The teachers thought it was a great joke, and gave me some work to do until I grew up. At eight years I fell off my horse and broke my leg, but my childhood was fairly uneventful otherwise.

The first time I was brought home as a baby, no one recognised me. This was not surprising because the nurses had mixed me up with the child over the road. The relatives all crowded around at first, although they soon lost interest when the real nappy work began.

Later, when I leave school, I would like to be a taxidermist or maybe a taxi driver, but for the moment I am enjoying life to the full. There have been changes which I can see have matured my character in the last year, but I still think that I was a typical Aussie child with no real hang-ups for most of my childhood.

The teenage years are often considered to be the most difficult in a person's life. This was probably true for me when I was becoming interested in girls. It all turned out to be very frustrating because they pestered me in Year 6 when I certainly was not interested, but when I did make the effort in Year 9, they had all developed other interests. The lesson I learned from this stage of my life was that you should be yourself, otherwise people will see that you are only putting on a front.

Now I am in my final years of school, which have been generally happy ones. Probably the most important thing at this stage of your life is to have supportive friends, which I think I have. Looking back over my life, I see several failures and embarrassments, such as when I waited at the wrong church for Jan's wedding, but on the whole there have been enough successes. In other words, life has been fun up to this point in time.

Narrative Essay C

Once upon a time there was a Mama and a Papa and a little baby boy. They were living a happy life on a tropical island in the middle of nowhere. Soon, along came a little baby girl. Her name was Lisa Jane. She went on to travel the world and back again, living a happy existence.

Her family was a very close-knit one. They did a lot together and were supportive. Her family consisted of her mother, a teacher, her father, also a teacher, and a brother two years older than herself. He was also born in Nauru. A brother, Shane, seven years younger than Lisa, was the only one of the children born in Australia. Lisa also had a sister, Kamala, adopted from Sri Lanka. Nine years younger than herself, Kamala was the baby of the family. Of late her pets have included a Collie dog answering to Larni, a stray cat, Nina, and a budgie, Thursday.

Lisa had travelled much in her life, having been born in Nauru. After six months she moved back to Albury, Australia. At the age of two her family moved again to Balldale, a small country town in New South Wales. This is where she 'grew up'. After the birth of her younger brother Shane, they headed off for mystical South-East Asia, where she lived with her family in Malaysia for three years. While there, they travelled to many other countries, including Thailand, Indonesia, Hong Kong, Sri Lanka, Singapore and most of Malaysia. On returning to Australia, they moved to Albury where they have remained ever since.

Lisa has many dreams that she wishes to fulfill. Travelling to Canada later this year as an exchange student is one of these dreams. She wishes to follow a career in physiotherapy and further travel the world. Lisa, since coming into this world, has had a happy life with a caring family. She has learnt much from her travels and wishes to continue them and her education. She also wishes to learn about and help the world and its people as much as possible.

CHAPTER 5
The Discursive Essay

> A discursive essay sets out to explore its topic by looking at it from different viewpoints, often using a 'for and against' approach.

A discussion does not take sides. The primary role of the discursive essay is to investigate the range of views relevant to its topic. You should present these views fairly, no matter what strong personal views you hold. Take the case of a computer fanatic faced with the question: 'Discuss the claim that computers do more harm than good'. He or she would be obliged to present the points *for and against* computers in a fair and balanced way. Although a balanced discussion does not take sides, it should still come to some conclusion at the end. At the close of the investigation, the different viewpoints may be weighed against each other, and an informed summing up made. Using the above example, the computer fanatic may have found that, *on balance*, computers were worthwhile.

You should plan your discursive essay by *determining the balance of views at the planning stage*, so that a fair exploration is made possible. It is important that you stand back from an issue and look at it from all angles. If you do allow strong personal feelings to rule your discussion, readers will not take your conclusions seriously because they will have been taken on a one-sided tour of the topic.

Trace the formation of the discursive essay below. Watch for the way the plan determines the balance of viewpoints to be explored.

Example 10

(Discuss) the claim that <u>computers</u> do <u>more harm than good</u>.

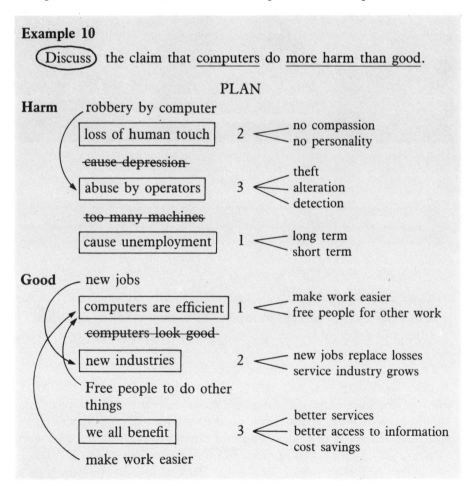

THE DISCURSIVE ESSAY   37

This question specifies two opposing views: 'harm' and 'good'. As equal marks will be awarded to each part, equal time has been awarded to each view. Much of the shaping of the essay has already been completed through the familiar steps:

- ANALYSE THE QUESTION

- SELECT RELEVANT POINTS
- DECIDE STATUS OF POINTS

- ORDER POINTS
- MAKE SUBDIVISIONS

Note that half of our operational steps are taken up with the production of the plan; the other half with writing. These first three steps will become particularly important where longer, more complicated questions are set for discussion.

Now see how the plan is used to shape the essay.

Example 10 (continued)

(Discuss) the claim that computers do more harm than good.

Paragraph topics contribute to the introduction.

> Our reliance on computers has brought problems as well as benefits. Loss of employment, the impersonal nature of computers and the dangers of abuse by operators, on the one hand, must be weighed against the efficiency of the machines, the new industries created and the benefits which flow to all, on the other.

Harm

cause unemployment
- short term
- long term

Loss of employment opportunities has been one obvious effect of our increasing use of computers. In the short term, this can be seen in the reduced need for clerical workers, particularly in large companies. In the long term, there will be demands for operators, analysts and so on, but these are increasingly specialised jobs. While new opportunities have surfaced, the big loser has been the worker with few skills.

loss of human touch
- no compassion
- no personality

Computers have no human touch. Machines dealing in numbers show no compassion towards people, and virtually exclude humans from most operations, especially in government departments. Although some computers have a 'voice', this is only a token form of personality. The result of this is a sterile, dehumanised workplace for employees.

abuse by operators
- theft
- alteration
- detection

This comment warns the reader of the importance of the point of the paragraph.

This comment links the paragraph with the question and tells the reader how important the point is.

The danger of abuse of computers by operators is a very real one. Theft of funds from large companies and banks is a major problem. Alteration of data in computerised records <u>is another, perhaps more insidious, hazard</u>. Detection of criminals who use such methods is made more difficult by the number of legitimate users. Illegal access by hackers is a further complication. Although companies and governments are aware of these problems and use sophisticated methods of protection and detection, the balance has not always been in their favour. <u>The potential for criminal abuse of computers is thus a harmful aspect of their use.</u>

THE DISCURSIVE ESSAY

Good

computers are efficient
— make work easier
— free people for other work

new industries
— new jobs replace losses
— service industry grows

we all benefit
— better services
— better access to information
— cost savings

This statement prepares the reader for the summing up process.

The middle section of this conclusion summarises the result of the discussion undertaken in the body paragraphs.

A clear judgement is made. This decision is justified by what has gone before, and answers the question.

On the positive side, computers are clearly efficient. Jobs have been made easier by the elimination of many long, repetitive tasks such as the storage, retrieval and cross-referencing of information. Considerable time saving has been achieved, especially in large government departments. A significant advantage is that people released from repetitive work are free to perform in areas such as planning and decision making. Efficient computer technology has thus had important spin-off effects for the community.

Computerisation has spawned a wide range of new industries. Employment opportunities in retailing, software, systems analysis and services have helped replace losses caused by the use of technology. The services sector has grown substantially, particularly in the information and consultancy fields. While computers have closed some doors, they have opened others.

Directly or indirectly, we all benefit from the work of computers. We are given better services by government and business. Professionals have better access to information, such as medical cases for doctors, and criminal records for police. These efficient services mean savings of time and money. On the national level, we are able to achieve more of our objectives as a result of the computer networks.

Weighing the good against the harm done by computers, it can be seen that the technology is a double-edged sword: loss of employment in one area is balanced by growth in another; and the potential for criminal abuse is balanced by improving protection and detection. Perhaps most significantly, the computer has freed human energies for use in other areas of need. Thus, while there are drawbacks, computers clearly do more good than harm.

Exercise 9: Planning a discursive essay

(1) Look at the introduction of the essay given in example 10. Has the discussion been prejudiced or balanced at this stage? Find evidence to support your response.

(2) What can you say about the direction of the essay, having read only the introduction?

(3) Does each body paragraph deal with material specified for it in the plan? Does each one have a topic sentence and a concluding sentence?

It is important that each body paragraph is seen as one step in a whole journey, rather than as an isolated island of information. The element that best helps you to link your paragraphs is the *comment* or observation you make in each paragraph. These comments need not necessarily be only in the concluding sentences, but they must make links with the question and with other paragraphs.

(4) Read the conclusion of the essay. What functions are the following statements performing in the paragraph?
   (a) 'it can be seen that technology is a double-edged sword'
   (b) 'perhaps most significantly'
   (c) 'while there are drawbacks'
   (d) 'computers clearly do more good than harm'.

The question asking writers to discuss the 'good' and 'harm' done by computers is very specific. Here, the different viewpoints have been spelt out to writers. This will not always be so; the question could well have been: 'Discuss our use of computers'. In this case, the two sides of the issue are implied rather than stated outright. Think carefully about your questions, particularly the brief ones, because these often imply that certain approaches be taken. Remember why we have the step: *analyse the question*.

Exercise 10: Constructing a discursive essay

Your discursive essay question is: 'Discuss our use of cars'. The following points may be useful to you during your planning operations. Feel free to add or eliminate points in order to draft a relevant plan.

- convenience
- not restricted by schedules
- freedom

- overcome distance barrier
- allow us to visit Aunt Nora in Dalgety
- fast method of travel
- comfortable
- saves us time
- efficient
- relatively cheap to run
- good back-up network
- air pollution
- we can pick our favourite colour in cars
- high death toll
- many injuries
- the wheels come off at high speeds
- more stressful life with cars
- faster pace of life
- we plan life around cars
- space taken for cars
- life is no longer at a human pace

Once you have drafted your plan, continue through the remaining steps to construct a drafted discursive essay.

CHECKLIST

- Have I determined a balance of views at the planning stage?
- Has my introduction prepared a prejudiced or balanced discussion for the reader?
- Does each body paragraph have a topic sentence and a concluding sentence?
- Have the discussion points been weighed up in the conclusion?
- After the weighing of viewpoints, have decisions been arrived at in the conclusion?

Additional Discursive Essay Questions

(1) Discuss the major environmental issues facing Australia today.
(2) Discuss the issues raised by IVF (in-vitro fertilisation) programs in Australia.
(3) Discuss the main changes Australia has seen since European settlement.

> The *discursive* essay question set for each of the three essays was: 'Discuss the effects that television has had on us'.

Discursive Essay A

There are several significant effects that television has on us, both harmful and beneficial. Some effects are obvious but others are more subtle. The benefits are that programs inform and educate us, while harmful effects can be seen in the way television can affect family life, cause addiction and present biased or misleading information.

The benefits that television brings us in the form of news and current affairs are easily demonstrated. The world is brought into our lounge rooms through the use of satellites, and we are kept up to date on developments wherever news is in the making. It must be acknowledged that there are dangers associated with this race for news: the shocking and the sensational become part of our children's television diet. It is nothing to see bodies in the streets, even on the ABC, and we become desensitised to the horrors of the world. The achievements of such an efficient service must, nonetheless, be recognised.

Other benefits include information that it is in the public's interest to know. Investigative television, such as 'Four Corners' and 'The Investigators', has had an important impact on the standards which Australians set themselves. The Fitzgerald Enquiry in Queensland was partly the result of such television work. Despite the successes, there may be problems with televised investigation that is too intrusive, such as during high-profile court cases. A balance must therefore be found whereby both public and private interests are protected.

The educational value of television has been demonstrated through highly respected shows such as 'Sesame Street', 'Quantum' and 'Living Planet'. Children's literacy and numeracy have clearly been helped by 'Sesame Street'. Television is an excellent medium through which to teach skills. The video industry has recognised this and we have benefited from this access to education which may otherwise have been unavailable. There are certainly some strong educational roles performed by television.

On the harmful side, television often dominates family life and stifles real communication. In cases where both parents work, there may be little time for the whole family to be together, and with television, conversations are usually about the shows rather than about the family. In this way television is a thief of family time.

For some people, television offers a very real chance of addiction. Shows such as 'General Hospital' and 'Days of Our Lives' may even take some viewers out of the real world, particularly where the viewers' lives are already dreary or hopeless. On a more general level, the very habit of watching television every day can have a powerful impact on the way people use their time. This is a particularly harmful and insidious effect of the medium.

Perhaps one of the greatest dangers of television is the way biased or misleading presentation of information damages people's reputations. Recent court cases have brought complaints of 'trial by media', and some current affairs presenters do set out to lead viewers by the nose. Whether viewers are being led to the truth is not always a matter of any consequence. To counter this, viewers must be prepared to use their own judgement, and must not allow themselves to be misled.

There is no doubt that television is a powerful thing; its effects on us are wide-ranging. Some of its strongest influences are also those least recognised by viewers, especially the way it moulds our opinions and steals our time. While accepting the substantial and desirable role of television in the areas of education and information, we must guard against the excesses of some presenters, and be prepared to use our judgement where theirs has failed. Television may seem to be a benevolent giant, but it is really a sly monster against which we must constantly be on our guard.

Discursive Essay B

The introduction of television to Australia thirty years ago was thought to be a great advance in technology. Yet today, people are realising that along with advantages such as enjoyment, education and a source of vital information, television also has a harmful side linked with health problems and obsession.

Noticeable health problems can result from excessive television. Instead of exercising and spending time outside in the fresh air, people become glued to the TV screen. They begin inhaling stale air and their blood does not circulate efficiently. This causes cholesterol difficulties or obesity. Thus, television can become extremely dangerous to a person's health.

Obsession is another harmful effect of television. When a person actually becomes addicted, friends and family are replaced by the TV. Eventually, human company becomes rare and the art of conversation is lost. It is also possible that people become so involved in the television world that they believe it is reality. Sometimes, they even perform violent acts to imitate their hero, while all the time thinking it is permissible. This is a very frightening aspect of television.

On the positive side, we receive a great deal of enjoyment from watching movies, comedies or a mini-series. Our minds are taken off everyday worries and we are allowed to relax. Becoming involved in the fantasy world is an excellent way to unwind and make ourselves at ease.

Television is also a reliable source of information as we are told of world-wide current affairs, either disasters or fortunate occurrences. Such things as sport, weather predictions and advertisements are broadcast, allowing us to keep up to date with the latest events.

Knowledge is also gained from television. Educational programs like 'Play School' and 'Sesame Street' teach children as well as provide entertainment, whilst documentaries help educate adults in serious matters. Therefore society benefits from this.

Looking at the good and the harmful side of television, we should be able to see that, when used wisely, it is very advantageous. So, while there are disadvantages, it is clear that television is more beneficial than harmful to us.

Discursive Essay C

The effect that television has on people in today's society is enormous. Not only does it affect us mentally, but physically as well. In this essay I will attempt to discuss the good points as well as the obvious problems associated with television.

Television is one of the most remarkable inventions made this century, and is a very important part of our lives. Although generations before us have lived quite well without television, today's society would be far from what it is now without it.

Firstly, education would be different. Schools would not have video resources and young children would not be able to watch the various children's shows now available to help them learn and understand.

Television should be used as a way to relax and relieve tension and stress. But, in general, people these days have grown more lazy since television has been introduced into the home. People are now able to sit and watch the wide variety of television shows available, instead of being outside getting sufficient exercise. Because of this, growing weight problems have occurred as well as, for some people, lack of sleep, which is also unhealthy.

If not for the television and its industry, many people working as actors, directors, scriptwriters and camera men, just to name a few, would not be in that line of work. Therefore if television was not around, maybe the unemployment statistics would be sky-high! These actors also have a strong influence on various people who devotedly follow their favourite stars' lives each episode of the soap operas. Many television shows have been blamed for the suicides and murders of young people recently. People who get so involved in movies and television and relate them back to real life can be affected mentally, and in some cases people do become violent. This is obviously a problem, but not a major everyday problem.

When we look back and review the effect that television has had on us, we see that it is a practical part of our lives. It provides us with entertainment and enjoyment and although it has minor drawbacks, it is an appliance that we cannot live without.

* * *

Each of the three essay types examined so far gives the topic as a starting point but few guidelines are given. This allows you the freedom to be creative, imaginative and to explore ideas.

The next three types of essay, *expository, analytical* and *argumentative*, usually involve specified material and a particular task is given. These essays require a logical, thoughtful response.

The three steps of question analysis, planning and writing apply to all three types, but there is further work required where a *source* is involved.

Before planning the essay you should:
- make sure you understand the source material
- be able to summarise what was said
- work out the importance of ideas presented and the strength of the evidence used to support them.

CHAPTER 6
The Expository Essay

> An expository essay sets out to explain something to the reader. Its main purpose is to increase the reader's understanding of the topic.

An expository essay may explain, for instance, how something works, what conditions existed at a particular time in history or how something is done.

Before you can begin to explain something to the reader, you must have a sound knowledge of your material and know exactly what you aim to explain.

THE EXPOSITORY ESSAY

The ordering of this material and the clarity of your explanation are crucial elements in this type of essay. Too often, students assume that the reader will always follow and understand. This is not necessarily the case; it is up to you to prepare the reader's path.

It may be useful to assume that the reader knows nothing about the topic. This will help you to think carefully about your choice of technical terms and about the amount of detail you are asking the reader to take in.

Only information that is essential to your explanation should be included. This is a difficult area for many writers. The word 'essential' should be kept in mind when you are choosing which material to include in your essay and which you should leave out.

There should be a logical sequencing of information. You should decide on the sequence at the planning stage.

Finally, the expository essay should be drafted where time permits.

Summary
1. Know your material.
2. Know what you are trying to explain.
3. Assume that the reader knows nothing about the topic.
4. Plan your information in a logical order.
5. Eliminate any information not essential to your explanation.
6. Draft your essay where time permits.

Example 11

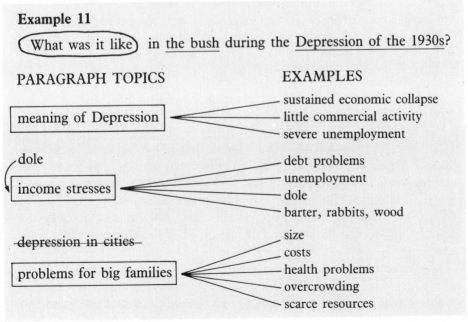

continues ▶

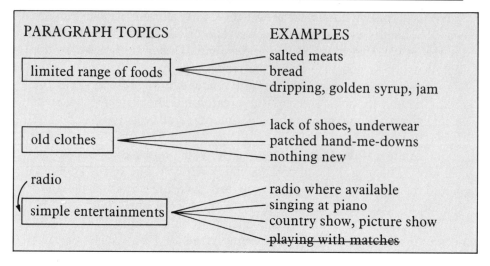

This question is an open one. It is up to the writer to decide what subject matter is worthy of inclusion. The plan shows two levels of detail: paragraph topics and examples. However, there is room for further subdivision. For example, 'debt problems' and 'health problems' are more general than 'lack of shoes' and 'singing at piano'. On the other hand, a high degree of specific comment on each topic is not required because the question really asks for a general impression of conditions. When planning an answer to such a question, you must keep the overall picture in mind: what it was like and which main topics deserve coverage. At the same time, you should include enough specific detail to support your points and satisfy the reader's interest. Finally, you must test the plan against the terms of the question.

Now read the completed essay.

(What was it like) in the bush during the Depression of the 1930s?

The Great Depression was a period of sustained economic collapse. For most Australians, this meant little commercial activity and severe unemployment. The Depression had a deep impact on all people in the bush, although it affected some families more dramatically than others. There were major pressures on the family unit: on incomes, on the supply of food and clothes, and on the types of entertainment that were available.

Considerable pressures were brought to bear on families, particularly the larger ones. Those struggling to keep ten or more children faced a limited food supply and the danger of killer diseases such as diphtheria and gastro-enteritis. A lack of resources such as bedding commonly resulted in wheat bags being used for blankets by children. The results of poverty and overcrowding may be partly measured in the number of deaths amongst children.

Stresses on the incomes of bush families varied according to ownership of land and to the degree of indebtedness. The combination of debt and unemployment forced many farming families from their land, after which the dole was the only choice for many. Bartering goods, for instance grain for flour, was one option for some. Other income was sought from the sale of rabbit skins and wood. The constant uncertainty and threat of poverty proved a great frustration for the larger families in the bush.

Limited incomes meant that the range of foods available was also limited. The lack of proper refrigeration frequently meant that any affordable meats had to be salted. Families under stress relied on home-made bread, jam, dripping or perhaps golden syrup or honey. Probably the strongest feature of bush food at this time was its monotony.

Clothing problems, especially for children in battling families, were keenly felt. Patched hand-me-downs were common, and younger children often had to go without shoes. Some items, such as underwear, became luxuries that only the elder children of struggling families could even hope to have. It was the children who often bore the brunt of the clothing crisis.

Bush entertainments were simple in the depressed early 1930s. Radios were becoming available for those who could afford them, but most entertainments required payment, which precluded the involvement of big families. For children from battling households, the country show was a time to window shop rather than spend. Town picture shows were fine if you could sneak in as a youngster. Around the home, adults sang around a piano where possible. Unlike today, bush entertainments revolved around the involvement of the whole family.

The Depression years in the bush were certainly stressful for many, and brought adult pressures to bear on children in large families. The uncertainty of incomes and the crisis of indebtedness loomed ominously over households. Despite the bleak outlook, simple pleasures were enjoyed and a hardy resourcefulness evolved in the growing children soon to face World War II.

One of the most common problems for the expository writer is the poor sequencing of information. Suppose you were asked to explain how to drive a manual car. If you launched into the operation of the controls before explaining the function of those controls, you would confuse rather than inform the reader. A more logical ordering of paragraphs in the planning stage would help rectify this problem.

Even where paragraph order has been carefully prepared, the way information is presented *within paragraphs* is still very important. Clear and simple topic sentences are vital, especially where detailed or complex material is to be explained. If you had to explain how to drive a manual car, how would you explain the role of the brakes or the instrument panel? On a more difficult level, how would you describe the function of the gears? Compare your explanations with those of other students and listen to their comments. If you assume that the reader knows nothing of the topic, this should remind you to keep your topic sentences simple.

Do not wait for an essay question in order to practise your skills of exposition. Try drafting expository paragraphs that explain everyday items to an audience not familiar with them. 'Test-drive' these explanations on other readers or, later, re-read them yourself. Remember to listen to the advice of other readers where possible, and be prepared to make changes for the sake of clarity.

Exercise 11: Planning an expository essay
This first exercise only requires plans for each expository question. Take the time to draft each plan carefully so that logic and clarity are preserved.
(1) Explain *either* (a) the greenhouse effect *or* (b) how a democratic government works.
(2) Explain *either* (a) how a bicycle works *or* (b) the conditions under which convicts lived in the early years of the penal settlement at Sydney.

Examine your plans, paying close attention to the sequence of information in each case. Does each plan provide a clear and logical explanation?

Exercise 12: Constructing an expository essay
This question requires you to draft both the plan and the essay.
Explain *either* (a) the role of a police force in a democracy *or* (b) the conditions under which Australian soldiers fought at Anzac Cove during the Gallipoli Campaign.

CHECKLIST
- Did I understand clearly what I had to explain?
- Did I assume that the reader knows nothing of the topic?
- Did I plan for a logical sequencing of information?
- Are my topic sentences clear and simple?
- Where possible, have other readers tested my explanation?

Additional Expository Essay Questions
(1) What functions do the corrective services perform in Australia?
(2) Explain how to operate a motor cycle.
(3) Explain why the earth's ozone is at risk, and why Australians should be particularly wary of the dangers.

The *expository* essay questions set for each of the three essays was: 'Explain how to drive a manual car'.

Expository Essay A

To drive a manual automobile, you must understand the many procedures involved. I will explain to you how to start the vehicle, then how to take off, change gears, use your indicators, turn corners and, finally, I will show you how to stop your vehicle safely.

After we have entered the vehicle and we feel comfortable, it is time to start the automobile. To do so, we must place the gearshift into first (refer to top of gear knob on gearshift). When doing this, the clutch must be in. After putting it in gear we must then press in the clutch again and start the vehicle using the key. (Be careful not to rev the motor too much.) After this has been done, we may start our drive.

To start our drive we must slowly release the clutch while slowly pressing the accelerator in. (Be sure to keep the revs at a steady pace.)

When you have completely released your foot from the clutch you may then keep pressing the accelerator to gain more speed.

When the revs reach a high level (about four to five thousand revs per minute) it is then time to change into a higher gear. To do so, we must push in the clutch and let the accelerator out. It is then time to move the gearshift into second gear (refer to the gearshift knob). When the gearshift has been placed into second, we may then release the clutch while pressing in the accelerator; this procedure is used for changing both up and down gears.

Now that we feel comfortable with the gears, it is time to attempt the corner. As we approach the corner we must use our indicators to signal to other drivers which way we are going. After doing this we must then start to slow down and change into a lower gear (second or third). This will enable us to take the corner with complete control. When we reach the corner we can safely turn.

Now that we have taken the corner safely and completed most of our obstacles, it is time to pull over to the side of the road. To do this safely, we use our indicators and slow down, using both the brake and the clutch. The use of the clutch here prevents the car from stalling. When we are completely stopped on the side of the road, we may turn the engine off using the key. We may then remove our feet from the pedals.

Driving a manual car will become an everyday thing once you get used to the gears, indicators, road rules, taking off and pulling up. These procedures will become second nature after a little practice. The only thing you need to become a safe driver is control of your car at all times. All these things put together will make your driving experience a whole lot easier.

Expository Essay B

Driving a car involves an understanding of many points. To be a competent driver, you must understand the rules of the road and car maintenance as well as how the car operates. It is important to tackle every aspect of driving before getting behind the wheel. Although the layout of automobiles differs with each model, the position of the essentials is similar. From the driver's seat, the steering wheel is in front. The gear change is either on the floor by your left hand, in which case it is called a floor shift, or on the left-hand side of the wheel, which is called a column shift.

Pedals on a car are the same on all manuals. From left to right, they are: clutch, brake and accelerator. The clutch disengages the engine from the wheels. Brakes are on all four wheels to slow or stop the vehicle's motion. The accelerator governs the revs of the motor.

The handbrake is located either between the seats or under the steering column. The gears on an automobile enable the vehicle to tackle different gradients whilst maintaining a rev speed comfortable to the engine. There are usually four forward gears and one reverse. First is used when going from a standstill. Second is the follow-on, or for steep hills. Third is the next in sequence, then fourth, the cruising gear. Refer to the diagram on the gear stick for the position of gears. When changing gears, listen to the engine pitch; when it is high, change up to the next gear. Change by depressing the clutch with your left foot and let off some accelerator with your right. Engage the next gear. Now let the clutch off whilst pushing the accelerator. The same sequence applies to changing down through the gears.

The lights are located on a panel under the wheel. They have a high beam (used in dark conditions where there are no other cars around) and a low beam (used in traffic). The indicators are behind the wheel and move on a stick. The horn is on the wheel. Wipers are on a binnacle near the indicators.

Dials or readouts on a car include the speedo, (giving velocity in km/h), the odometer (giving total distance travelled), the tachometer (giving revs per minute), the temperature gauge and the petrol gauge.

The most important thing to remember on the road is to obey the rules. Road rules may be found in the Motor Transport Authority booklet, but in all cases you should obey the signs and pointers around you.

Many car owners have experienced the problem of their cars not starting. For all mechanical problems you should call your roadside repairer, such as the RACV and the NRMA. They will endeavour to remedy any problems you have. Bigger problems are usually referred to a mechanic.

When buying a second-hand car, always look for the obvious signs of deterioration. The car should have a pink slip, a certificate of proof that the car is roadworthy. Even so, the car should be test-driven so that you can get the feel of it.

Now you should have grasped the fundamentals of driving and should be on your way to becoming a competent driver. Never become careless, and keep all your skills in good practice. This way you will stay a good and safe user of our roads.

Expository Essay C

Driving a manual car is complicated at first, but can become easier as your knowledge of methods, laws, instruments and controls increases.

There are many basic things which must be considered all at once while driving: a knowledge of the car's instruments and the laws and methods vital to safe driving.

One of the main considerations of driving a manual car concerns these basic things. First you need a manual car, a driver, a place to drive, and some knowledge of the controls, laws and instruments. You must have these things if a manual car is to be driven successfully. Therefore, a learner's first considerations are these basic needs.

Because there are so many instruments and controls in a manual car, a knowledge of where they are and how they help is essential. They can be divided up into four groups: safety equipment, foot controls, hand controls and gauges. Safety equipment, made for the driver's safety, can be found everywhere on the car. Seat belts are connected just behind the seats, and the handbrake can be found under the dash or on the floor on either side of the driver's seat. There is more safety equipment that is not really necessary for actual driving. The foot controls can be found on the floor of the car. These include, from left to right: clutch pedal, brake pedal and accelerator. As expected, all hand controls are within arm's reach on the dash or by the sides of the seat. The most important are the steering wheel, on the dash, the gear stick, usually on the floor, and switches for various things, which are found on the dash. All gauges are found on the dash in front of the driver.

When you know where all the controls are, you should learn what each one does and what it is used for. The safety equipment is built for the passengers' and the car's safety. The seat belts restrain the passengers from going through the windscreen, and locks protect the car against theft. The clutch is used to disengage the motor while stopping and changing gears. The brake and accelerator are used for stopping, and controlling the motor's running speed. There are various hand controls, but the most important are the steering wheel (used to steer the car), the gear stick (used to change gears), and switches, such as the indicator switch which is used to warn other drivers that the car will be turning. The gauges show the driver what is happening in the car and warn the driver about any faults which the car may have.

When a knowledge of the car's controls has been gained, it is then possible for the learner driver to actually begin to drive. The first thing to do is to hop in, buckle up the seat belt and check some of the safety equipment such as the rear view mirrors on the windscreen and on the doors. Then, start the car after making sure that it is in neutral gear. Then, by depressing the left-most pedal, the clutch, disengage the motor and select the desired gear, either first or reverse. First must always be selected when taking off or going very slowly, in order to use the engine's power most efficiently. Then, as the car speeds up, the next highest gear is selected. These gears can be engaged by moving the gear stick to a certain position for each gear. A label can be found either on the gear stick or near it, showing the various gears and their positions. Once the required gear is found, the clutch must be let out to engage the motor. However, if the motor's speed varies greatly from the wheel speed, then the clutch must be let out slowly while 'revs' are applied with the accelerator. This happens when taking off. The driver should carefully listen to the motor at all times. If it sounds too high or low, then a more appropriate gear should be chosen. The steering wheel is used at all times by the driver to steer. To slow down, the driver can either slowly work down through the gears or apply the clutch pedal and press lightly on the brake.

There are many laws and methods that drivers must follow while driving on public roads for safety's sake. Some road rules have been made to protect the public and the driver. For example, you must indicate before turning and restricting your speed and a driver who is found disobeying these rules will be penalised. Some complications involved in the driving of a manual car cannot be totally avoided. Almost all cars can break down and overheat. Therefore, it is best to have such things as spare tyres and jacks, and insurance against accidents is recommended.

Driving a car is quite complicated, but can be made easier by learning all the road rules and the controls of a manual car. Because a knowledge of laws, controls and requirements plays such an important role in the driving of a manual car, these things must all be accounted for when you learn to drive. If all of these rules are followed and considerations taken into account, the driving of a manual car can be both easy and safe. Unfortunately, complications such as breakdowns and tyre blowouts cannot be avoided by the most aware and careful driver, so it is best to be prepared as well.

CHAPTER 7
The Analytical Essay

> The analytical essay separates its topic into parts in order to examine and understand it more fully.

It is important that you understand the requirements of the analytical essay. Firstly, you should separate the topic into its component parts just as a mechanic would do when analysing a mechanical problem. Secondly, each main part must be examined and its contribution to the whole must be determined (e.g., the role of the sparkplug in a misfiring engine). Finally, there must be some clear understanding of the whole based on the analysis of the parts (e.g., the relative importance of different parts of the engine as contributors to the misfiring problem).

Summary
1. Decide on the main elements to be analysed.
2. Determine the characteristics of each element and the effect of each on the problem.
3. Combine the findings on each element examined. What understanding of the whole problem has been gained?

An analytical question may not always present a problem. For example, 'Analyse the role of police in Australia' presents an issue rather than a problem. One of the dangers you face in answering this type of question, is substituting mere description for analysis. You must avoid this *in the plan*.

A plan for this question might include paragraph topics such as 'enforcing laws', 'maintaining order' and 'investigating crimes'. However, these would only lead to a description unless the plan also indicated, for instance, how successfully each role is performed. In other words, *an analytical plan should combine paragraph topics with point-form critical comment.*

Example 12

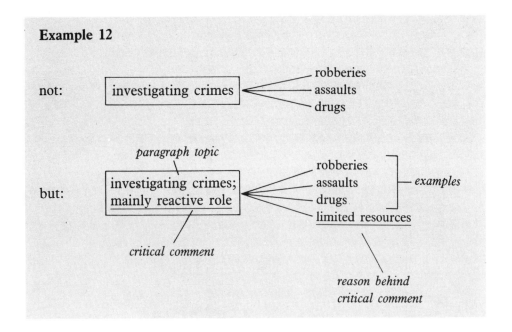

Now look at example 13 on the following pages. It shows how all the steps of analysis are applied to the topic 'Analyse the misfiring problem in this motor'.

58 ESSAY CLINIC

Example 13

Analyse the misfiring problem in this motor.

STEPS	POINTS	PARAGRAPHS
DECIDE THE MAIN ELEMENTS TO BE ANALYSED	~~gears~~ → electrical system; sparkplug; ~~clutch~~; fuel system; lubrication	Several aspects of this motor must be analysed if the fault is to be understood. The electrical system, the fuel system and the lubrication of the motor are the elements requiring close study.
DETERMINE THE CHARACTERISTICS OF EACH ELEMENT AND THE EFFECT OF EACH ON THE PROBLEM OR ISSUE	electrical leads not conducting well → an unreliable element of this motor; sparkplug dirty, corroded → definitely one cause of misfiring; lubrication operating smoothly → poses no threat to operation of motor	The electrical leads prove to be poor conductors of current. This is an unreliable element in the motor. The dirty and corroded sparkplug is definitely one cause of misfiring, and adds to the lack of reliability. Lubrication of the motor is operating smoothly. Moving parts are not in any danger from excessive friction or heat. This element poses no threat to the motor's operation

THE ANALYTICAL ESSAY

	fuel tank dirty, lines partly blocked ⎤→ contributing factor to erratic firing of sparkplug ⎦	The fuel system has two problems. Firstly, the tank is dirty and is thus a source of contamination. Secondly, the fuel lines are partly blocked. Both elements of the fuel supply contribute to the erratic firing of the sparkplug.
COMBINE THE FINDINGS ON EACH ELEMENT EXAMINED. WHAT UNDERSTANDING OF THE WHOLE PROBLEM OR ISSUE HAS BEEN GAINED?	a combination of factors contributes to loss of reliability lubrication not a factor both parts of the fuel supply contribute to the problem electrical system, especially sparkplug, contributes to the problem.	The motor misfires because of a combination of factors, each of which contributes to a loss of reliability. Although lubrication was not a factor, both parts of the fuel supply, the electrical system and the sparkplug in particular, combined to cause the misfiring problem.

Exercise 13: Planning an analytical essay
Now it is time for you to try your hand at analysis. This first exercise requires only a plan in response to each question. Take the time to draft plans that will combine paragraph topics with critical comment.
(1) Analyse the role of police in Australia.
(2) Analyse the impact of pollution on the earth.
Examine both plans closely. Is each one analytical rather than descriptive?

Exercise 14: Constructing an analytical essay
This exercise requires you to draft both the plan and the essay.
- Analyse the impact television has had on the lives of Australians.

CHECKLIST
- Have I decided the main elements to be analysed?
- Have I made critical comment on each of these?
- Have I considered my findings and made broader comment on the whole?
- Is my response concerned with analysis rather than description?

Additional Analytical Essay Questions
(1) Analyse the drug problem in Australia.
(2) Analyse the systems of waste disposal in your city or town.
(3) Analyse the effects that the home video industry has had on Australian society.

ANALYTICAL ESSAYS FOR EVALUATION

> The *analytical* essay question set for each of the three essays was: 'Analyse the role of the police in Australia'.

Analytical Essay A

The police in Australia have several roles in the community, which are carried out with varying degrees of success. The main roles of the police force are to protect life and property, to enforce laws introduced by governments, to deter would-be criminals and to solve crimes.

The primary role of any police force should be to protect life and property. In this country, this aim has been achieved to a high degree in most areas. However, because of vast distances, some remote communities are left to protect themselves. This role of the police is vital to members of society who are vulnerable and unable to protect themselves, for example the very young and the very old. Lack of manpower in larger cities has often made this goal difficult to achieve, but the police have generally been successful.

Enforcing laws introduced by parliamentarians is another role for the police. Enforcing some laws may over-ride the need to enforce others. The recent case of the rebel egg farmer who did not conform to the appropriate laws and was evicted and had his chickens slaughtered illustrates the way the animal protection laws may be over-ridden. Enforcing the laws of parliaments is a role that is performed effectively by police, although police numbers determine that a priority system must be applied to requests for police help.

Solving crimes and convicting lawbreakers is an important aspect of police work. Success in this area has improved dramatically in recent years with the help of modern technology, such as forensic evidence and computerised records. Despite these advantages, the sharp increase in drug-related crimes has placed a heavy burden on police resources and manpower. Most metropolitan police forces have agreed that drug-related crimes are by far the biggest threat in today's society. A New

South Wales police commissioner said recently that they were fighting a losing battle against organised crime and drugs, and predicted that the situation would not improve until adequate funding was allocated to the police force.

Crimes committed also include those done by police. Recent revelations from the Fitzgerald Enquiry have demonstrated that police corruption, at all levels of the force, can have a devastating effect on the effectiveness and the morale of a state's police force. Similar problems in New South Wales and other states suggest that corruption is causing a significant loss of effectiveness in many areas of police activity. As a result of this, the public perception of police forces may have become more negative.

Today, police forces in Australia generally maintain a satisfactory level of law and order. The protection of life and property and the enforcement of most laws are carried out with competence and authority. However, in today's society, the police are facing an increasing occurrence of organised crime, from within and without, and unless governments act accordingly with funding and manpower, the situation will deteriorate.

Analytical Essay B

To analyse the role of police in Australia we must establish some individual roles that police take on, such as security and protection, the very important police rescue, the setting of an example on and off duty, and the encouragement of community involvement in police work.

Security and protection are generally the most common police roles that provide safety in Australia. Random breath testing is very well done in the eastern states, considering the lack of manpower. All over Australia, highway patrolling is executed with professionalism. Foot patrols are not as good as they could be; the main problem is the lack of manpower. Overall, security and protection are good.

The setting of an example to the public by police is lacking, as seen by the events of the Fitzgerald Enquiry in Queensland. The enquiry involved political and police corruption. Police behaviour in public is somewhere between fair and good, taking into account violence, corruption, and the few police in Australia who are involved in organised crime, especially in Queensland.

Police rescue is one of the more pleasing aspects of effective police work. Helicopter rescue is a lifesaving service. The Victorian Police use Medivac Helicopters, an example which other states are now following. Water rescue is very well conducted too. Many lives have been saved on the water when the sailors would otherwise have drowned.

Community involvement is attempted nationwide. Neighbourhood Watch is a program that encourages people to tell police if a crime is expected to be committed in a local neighbourhood. This has proved to be very efficient in stopping burglaries. Operation Noah is held a few times a year; it is the public's chance to tell police of any drug-related offences being committed.

'Crime Stoppers' is a nationwide television program which re-enacts crimes that have been committed. Because of the program, several escapees and murderers have been caught, which proves the show to be worthwhile. The involvement of the community in police work is proving to be worthwhile.

Overall, police work in Australia is done well, especially police rescue, community involvement and security and protection. The setting of an example to the public is two-sided, with corruption in Queensland letting the side down.

Analytical Essay C

The role of police in Australia covers several areas. Enforcing the law, finding and dealing with offenders, protecting people and maintaining order are the areas covered by police in Australia. They cover some of these areas better than others.

The major role of police in Australia is to enforce the law. The law can be broken up into two parts: criminal law and civil law. It is the role of police to enforce both parts of the law. Criminal law involves protecting the community from people who violate the safety and the interest of its members. Civil law deals with the rights of individuals, and aims to ensure that the individual is given protection from people who may wish to interfere with their rights. In both these areas the police do their best to uphold and enforce the law. However, criminal activity still occurs and some people have their rights infringed upon.

Finding and dealing with offenders against the law involves a number of things. Firstly, a crime must be investigated to discover the offender. After this, the offender is apprehended and arrested. Both these aspects are done well, considering they are not easy jobs. Last of all, the offender must be dealt with or punished in some way. This usually means a court hearing where a judge hands down a sentence. The police must deal with all these areas, although in the last area it is not often the police who deal with punishing offenders.

Another responsibility of the police is to protect people. In this, they try to prevent accidents and unnecessary deaths, although both of these are becoming more frequent. They also try to prevent criminal activity so that people, and their belongings, are kept from danger. This aspect, however, like the previous aspect, has not been dealt with completely successfully as crimes are constantly being committed. Protecting people is an extremely difficult task for the police to perform.

Maintaining order in society involves preventing riots and upholding a level of fairness and justice. Preventing riots eliminates some unnecessary violence and provides, to some extent, peace within a community. This is done rather well by police in Australia. Upholding a level of fairness and justice also helps maintain order. By preserving the status quo the people are kept content, knowing that in all circumstances they will be treated correctly and on a par with other people. The police also do this quite well, although not everyone feels that he or she is treated fairly.

The role of police in Australia covers a wide range of activities and responsibilities, and although some of these responsibilities are not performed as well as others, they are all carried out to a certain extent. Enforcing the law, finding and dealing with offenders, protecting people and maintaining order all combine to form the role of police in Australia.

CHAPTER 8
The Argumentative Essay

> An argumentative essay sets out to persuade the reader to hold a particular view by taking him or her through a series of reasoned steps to a logical conclusion.

A clear, persuasive argument has several important structural features. Firstly, it *defines* the key terms in the question. For instance, in the question 'Is random breath testing necessary for Australians?', the term 'random breath testing' would need to be given a specific meaning at the outset.

Secondly, it makes a short statement that sums up the case to be presented to readers; for instance 'random breath testing is necessary because it saves lives'. This statement is called a *contention* or *line of argument*.

Thirdly, the contention is *developed* and *supported* through steps that are reasonable and accessible to readers. The contention 'breath testing saves lives' could be developed through paragraph topics such as 'effect of alcohol on drivers', 'alcohol and road deaths', 'innocent victims' and so on. Within each of these paragraphs, relevant supporting evidence is offered. In this case, evidence could include specific effects of alcohol on drivers, comparative statistics on road deaths and the specific types of innocent victims at risk. A further task may be required in this part of the essay; this is the *countering* or *rebuttal* of other arguments opposing your own.

Finally, a persuasive argument must end with a *logical conclusion* — a judgement that it is now reasonable to make. In this example, a reasonable concluding statement could be: 'Random breath testing combats alcohol abuse by drivers and saves innocent lives, so it is essential that we have it'.

Summary

1. Define key terms in the question.

2. State your contention or main line of argument.

3. Develop your contention through body paragraph topics; support it with relevant examples. During this stage it may be necessary to rebut counter-arguments.

4. State the conclusions or judgements at which readers should logically arrive.

Refer to example 14 on pages 68–69, and follow each of the stages as the argument in favour of random breath testing is developed.

How soon did you have a clear idea of what would be argued? Did you find that the steps you followed were reasonable? Were the examples relevant to the case? Was the conclusion linked to the rest of the essay?

Arguments pose several problems for students. Surprisingly, many students do not tell readers what is to be argued at the outset. It is not good enough that the readers assume or guess your contention after reading half the essay. Make a bold statement at the start.

A second area of concern is that some writers argue both sides of a case, leaving the readers to make their own decisions at the end. This would be *discussion* rather than *argument*. Keep in mind that an argumentative essay requires you to argue the case for a particular point of view. You cannot 'sit on the fence'.

Thirdly, it is important that you do not ask the reader to make jumps in logic. When you link your evidence and comments to conclusions, the progression must seem to be a *reasonable* one. For example, it is reasonable to say that passengers, riders, drivers and pedestrians are put at risk by drunken drivers, and that random breath testing would help protect them. It is unreasonable to say that all passengers should be tested. There are texts that examine errors of logic; you may wish to read relevant sections of *Stands to Reason* by G.M. Hibbins or a similar text.

Summary

1. Do say what you will argue at the start of the essay.

2. Do develop your case in reasonable steps.

3. Do make conclusions that are supported by your evidence.

4. Do not sit on the fence.

5. Do not make sweeping, unsupported statements.

6. Do not make the reader jump in order to reach your conclusions.

Exercise 15: Planning an argumentative essay
Here are two questions that have caused considerable debate in Australia. Drafting only a plan in each case, prepare arguments for them.

(1) Should heroin be legalised in Australia?
(2) State the case for the re-introduction of capital punishment.

Examine both plans closely. Does each have a clear contention or main reason? Is each paragraph topic relevant to the contention? Are the examples directly supportive of the paragraph topics? What conclusions would it be reasonable to reach, given the material in each plan?

Example 14 Is random breath testing (necessary) for Australians?

STEPS	PLAN	PARAGRAPHS
DEFINE TERMS	random breath testing is: breath analysis of the blood-alcohol levels of motorists at police discretion	Random breath testing is the measurement of the blood-alcohol levels of motorists through breath samples taken at the discretion of the police. This testing is a simple, effective and necessary method of saving lives on our roads.
STATE YOUR CONTENTION	random breath testing saves lives	
DEVELOP YOUR CONTENTION THROUGH BODY PARAGRAPH TOPICS AND SUPPORT AT STRATEGIC POINTS WITH RELEVANT EXAMPLES	effects of alcohol on drivers — socially accepted drug; causes drowsiness, impairs judgement, affects co-ordination and reaction time (1984 figures)	Alcohol is a socially acceptable drug in Australia. As a depressant it can seriously affect drivers through drowsiness and impaired judgement, and through poor co-ordination and reaction time. In 1984 thirty-two per cent of Australian road accidents were related to alcohol.[1] The dangers of alcohol for Australian drivers are clear.
	alcohol and road deaths — NSW figures on deaths: before and after random breath resting	Many road deaths can be directly attributed to alcohol abuse. In New South Wales random breath testing has dramatically reduced fatalities from 653, January to June 1982, to 468 for the same period, 1983.[2] Since its introduction, preventative random breath

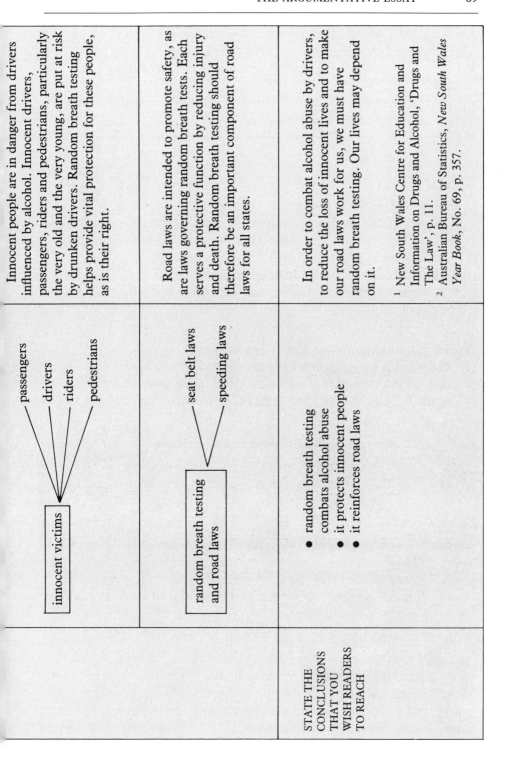

Exercise 16: Constructing an argumentative essay
The question below requires a fully drafted essay.
- There is a case for the logging of Australian native forests. Do you agree?

(This argument should involve some rebuttal of counter-arguments during the development of your case.)

---CHECKLIST---
- Have I defined key terms in the question?
- Have I stated my contention at the start of the essay?
- Have I developed this contention through the body paragraph topics and supported it with relevant examples?
- Have I rebutted the main counter-arguments?
- Are my conclusions logical and supported by what has gone before?

Additional Argumentative Essay Questions
(1) What is the case against bans on smoking in public?
(2) Has genetic research given science too much power?
(3) Is there a case for stricter censorship in Australia?

The *argumentative* essay question set for each of the three essays was: 'Should capital punishment be re-introduced in Australia?'

Argumentative Essay A

'A killer. A motive. A victim. A murder.' This is the type of plot used in the romanticised Sherlock Holmes books, set in the 1890s. Murder, then, seemed such a civilised affair. It was where the killer would spend weeks planning how to commit the murder and how to get away unseen. Such intricate planning today is virtually unheard of. It is more a case of hit and run or stalk, attack, rape then kill. Such acts of barbarism are almost a daily occurrence. It is barbarism that man is gradually returning to. Of course I only accuse elements of our society that perform these inhuman aggressive acts on their fellow man, but there are many such individuals throughout Australia.

It is not the act of aggression that we are concerned with, it is how we intend to deal with the aggressor. Australia does not have as high an incidence of murder as the United States, the murder capital of the world, but the figures are high enough for concern. Hardly a week goes by without us reading about some attack, whether it is in the form of rape or murder. The question is, if the government were to reinstate execution as a punishment for such crimes, would this stop the killings? In the United States, the executioner puts criminals to death, but the murders continue. Many of the most brutal attacks are performed by the mentally unstable, and to such individuals death has no meaning. To trace a killer one must think as they do. The state executioner brings death, but also more detailed investigations. If a person is falsely convicted he is, at present, sent to jail. If by chance the real culprit is discovered, he is released. Death is not so lenient. So capital punishment is not the answer to the murder problem in Australia.

Or is it? Someone who kills for the first time finds it hard. The second time he finds it easier. The third time even easier. After that his moral standards are non-existent, and killing becomes a natural function. Such a person could be stopped from killing the first time if the consequence of his capture was death.

Considering the amount of injustice in the justice system, the death sentence would recall the need for more thorough investigations, as there could not be a shadow of a doubt in the judge's mind as he passes the ultimate sentence. This would stop the aforementioned false convictions.

So, the death sentence is the answer to the murder problem in Australia. The essayist is either for or against, and should clearly state his or her point of view, but that is only one person's opinion. The only way to really find out if there is a case for capital punishment in Australia is to put the question to the populace, as it is we who are both the aggressors and the victims of aggression.

Argumentative Essay B

In Australia today, the incidence of horrific and repeated crimes against society has produced a great number of victims, both living and dead. If victims are to be put before the most serious offenders, and people are not to lose faith in the rule of law, capital punishment must be re-introduced in this country.

Capital punishment is the punishment of a crime by death. This has not been used in Australia since 1967. Since that time, however, the number of cold, savage crimes of murder has increased dramatically. This increase has been paralleled by a go-soft-on-offenders approach on the part of authorities, at great cost to victims.

The nature of the most serious crimes in Australia has changed significantly since the abolition of capital punishment, and a new category of murder now stands above all the rest. The Hoddle Street case, the Cobby murder and recent executions in Queensland demonstrate that massacres of innocent civilians do happen here, and that execution and torture are part of Australian crime now. One of the chilling implications of this is that we are no longer safe from the excesses we see in American society. The legal outcomes of our own cases are equally important in terms of the public's perceptions of justice, particularly where such serious offenders are eventually to re-enter the society from which innocent victims were cruelly taken.

In coping with the most serious murders, state governments have allowed the rehabilitation of offenders to overshadow their punishment, a trend that has been noted by an uneasy public. While murderers are groomed for re-entry to society, victims' families wait helplessly for a repeat of the original crime. At present in Australia, the most severe crimes against humanity are not met with the most severe punishments.

According to the civil rights lobby, capital punishment is legalised murder. No crime, they argue, is great enough to justify the offender's loss of life. In any case, there is the danger that the wrong person will be forced to pay that price. This line of reasoning places great value on the lives of serious offenders, but little value on the actual and potential victims. True, the courts are not perfect, and certainly public opinion is not always rational, but we must establish some absolute values and be prepared to defend them with the use of the severest penalties. Rarely, innocent people may be sent to their death under such a system, but there are far fewer of these than those innocents who die at the hands of re-offenders. Execution means the worst offenders lose their second chance, and the authority of law is enhanced in the public eye.

Here in Australia we take the rule of law for granted, but in America the lines are not so clearly drawn, especially in the wake of recent actions by vigilantes. There is clearly a danger that where courts are not permitted to apply the ultimate sanction, civilians may do it in the name of justice. If so, the status of the courts will suffer.

It would be foolish to deny that there are strong arguments for and against capital punishment, yet we should not deny that the terms of reference of the debate have changed since the 1960s, when massacres happened in other countries. Even with the risks, the worst murderers should earn the worst punishment, and we should not feel ashamed to punish such offenders. This approach will bring us as close as we are going to get to justice.

Argumentative Essay C

Capital punishment is the punishment of a crime by death. In Australia it has been abolished, the last hanging being in Victoria in 1967. Today, the death sentence is replaced by life imprisonment, which is generally twenty years minus parole. Some people do not think that life imprisonment is enough. They would prefer the defendant to be put to death. Would death be good enough?

After a serious crime, many people demand the death sentence, but this is purely an emotional reaction. These people are not thinking rationally about the issue; they are seeking revenge. The death sentence is as barbaric as the original crime; it is legalised murder. History has shown that capital punishment is not a deterrent. A person who plans a murder does not consider that he will be caught, and a crime of passion committed on the spur of the moment also does not take into account the consequences.

If someone is hanged and then later is found innocent, he has been murdered by society. A person jailed can be at least partly compensated for the ordeal. When a person is given the death sentence, his trauma spreads to his family and friends, and also the officials, the judge and the jury who send him to the gallows. This trauma is magnified many times if it is later proved that the accused was innocent.

Capital punishment is barbaric revenge that really achieves nothing. It is dangerous to administer the death sentence because it may be a big mistake that cannot be undone. The situation cannot be retrieved; it is a final decision. It is far better that five guilty men go free than one innocent man be executed.

In today's society, the crime rate has risen rapidly to the stage where some measure must be taken in order to deter criminals. There is definitely a case for capital punishment to be re-introduced to Australian society as it has the potential to dramatically reduce the crime rate. Perhaps the threat of such a severe punishment would give killers second thoughts about murdering, and civilians would live safely, knowing that murderers could not escape from jail to continue their killing. As well as this, hardworking, honest taxpayers would not be forced to pay for the upkeep of killers.

Introducing the death penalty would deter criminals and cut the crime rate. People would have second thoughts about committing murder, rape or child molestation if such a severe punishment was in existence. The thought of possible execution would in many cases destroy all criminal desire.

Re-introducing capital punishment would also mean that victims of such crimes as rape could live in safety and protection, knowing that their attackers could not possibly re-enter society. Knowing this would be a great comfort to many, and indeed the death penalty would give many people a chance to regain a normal lifestyle.

Hardworking, honest taxpayers are the people who pay for the upkeep of prisoners. It is they who feed and clothe the criminals. Society has absolutely no need for hardened criminals, so the government is simply wasting taxpayers' money in paying for the costs of keeping murderers alive.

Somewhere, however, we must draw the line between those who deserve merely a jail term and those who deserve a death sentence. It is criminals, such as rapists, child molesters, drug traffickers and cold-blooded killers that should be executed, whereas a jail sentence is sufficient for other offenders.

It should be kept in mind, however, that capital punishment is completely irreversible. Thus, if an executed prisoner is later found to be innocent, nothing can be done to remedy such a tragic situation. The knowledge of their innocence is hardly likely to ease the suffering of the family and friends of the victim. In effect, an innocent person has been legally murdered, therefore, must the executioner then be murdered for killing an innocent person?

In England, in the 1950s, Timothy Evans was hanged after being found guilty of a series of murders. After his death, it was proved that Evans was actually innocent, and a man by the name of Christie was the killer. Also, in the case of Lindy Chamberlain, a woman was found guilty and sentenced to life imprisonment for the murder of her baby daughter. Later, however, she was found to be innocent, and was released from prison with a pardon. If capital punishment had been in operation in this case, the dreadful mistake could not have been corrected, and much added suffering would have resulted.

Due to the fact that capital punishment would mean a reduction in taxes, an increase in the safety and security of many people, and an effective deterrent to many criminals, capital punishment is a favourable idea. There is definitely a case for it in Australia. If brought into existence, however, the law would have to be extremely clear that only those proved guilty beyond all possible doubt should be executed. This rule must be strictly adhered to, or innocent lives could be taken.

CHAPTER 9

Common Faults in Written Expression

AVOIDING ERRORS

The intention of this chapter is not to provide a systematic examination of grammar or structure, but to point out those errors most commonly made by students. The exercises are designed to help you identify and correct errors, and ultimately achieve a greater clarity and simplicity of expression.

Colloquialisms and Slang

Essays should be written in formal English. Therefore, there should be no short-cuts, such as contractions, nor any casual or slang expressions. For example, you can say 'firstly' but not 'for starters'. 'Could not' is acceptable, but not 'couldn't'. Another example: you can say 'without doubt' but not 'no mistake'.

Colloquial and slang expressions may appear in essays only as part of quotations that are relevant to the purpose of the essay.

Exercise 17: Avoiding colloquialisms and slang
Find formal expressions for the following:
(1) pretty good
(2) a fair bit
(3) caused a few hassles
(4) mucked up the plan
(5) just the thing
(6) finished up
(7) for a while there
(8) fair enough
(9) didn't kid herself
(10) wasn't really the best

Generally speaking, it is best to avoid informal expressions altogether, even in those instances where you 'admit' to informality by placing colloquialisms or slang in inverted commas. If you are unsure about the best way to convey your meaning to the reader, turn to a dictionary or thesaurus. You should not settle for a vague expression when a precise and appropriate one is close at hand.

Cliche

A *cliche* is a worn-out, over-used term that has lost its originality and impact. For instance, 'fall on deaf ears', 'a foregone conclusion' and 'in this day and age' are all cliches.

Exercise 18: Avoiding cliches
Find more original expressions for the following cliches:
(1) a whole new ballgame
(2) in this day and age
(3) tarred with the same brush
(4) to throw a spanner in the works

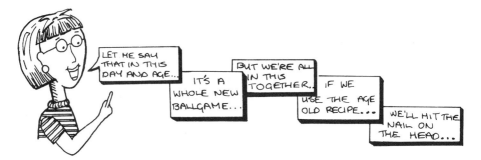

(5) to skate on thin ice
(6) as cool as a cucumber
(7) as dry as dust
(8) to hit the nail on the head
(9) in the same boat
(10) to leave someone in the lurch

Tautology

Tautology occurs when the same thing is said twice. Examples of this include 'look back in retrospect' and 'a three-part trilogy'.

Exercise 19: Avoiding tautology

Remove the tautology from each of the following sentences:
(1) The motorist was told to return back to the highway.
(2) Several dogs fought over one single bone.
(3) The bowler did not receive a favourable approval from the umpire.
(4) Voters in the election were faced with two alternative options.
(5) In my opinion, I think that the show should be repeated again after such a successful opening night.

Ambiguity

Ambiguity leaves readers with a choice of two or more meanings when only one is intended. For instance, if a doctor tells a patient that he 'will never be the same again' after an operation, the patient has no single meaning to rely on. Ambiguity is perhaps the most difficult problem to avoid for many students because simple errors, such as a misplaced comma, can mean the difference between a clear meaning and an ambiguous one.

Exercise 20: Avoiding ambiguity
Remove the ambiguity from each of the following sentences:
(1) The woman patted the dog as she ran past.
(2) An alligator was behind the animals waiting to feed.
(3) The politician held the koala and he urinated in front of the cameras.
(4) A band was at the station and the train went through it.
(5) Have you eaten mother?

Punctuation Errors

Essays often have long sentences that may contain several ideas or that involve complex explanations. If clarity of meaning is to be preserved, commas, apostrophes and quotation marks need to be used accurately and consistently. Commas are used to mark a natural pause in a sentence, to mark an aside from your main flow of ideas and to separate items in a list. Apostrophes are used to show ownership and to show contraction. Quotation marks are used when quoting the actual words that someone said, thought or wrote. Any punctuation associated with the words being quoted must appear *inside* the quotation marks.

Exercise 21: Using commas
Insert commas where necessary:
(1) On leaving camp George hastily donned an officer's coat.
(2) Outside the soldiers were resting.
(3) Gonzalez the athlete who had crawled across the continent was not impressed by the media coverage he received.
(4) 'Come hither Sir Horace' her eyes seemed to say.
(5) Haig although originally against the idea gave his consent.
(6) The fire destroyed all crops in the area most of the live-stock all of the timber structures and many farm vehicles.
(7) Having seen the destruction caused the lives lost and the cost incurred the generals decided to withdraw.
(8) 'I want to rule Europe' he told his staff 'but first we must win it'.

Exercise 22: Using apostrophes
Insert an apostrophe where necessary:
(1) Jane wants to clear the yard of Rovers collection of bones.
(2) Bills bike arrives today but he wont need it yet.
(3) Its wonderful to see the armadillo in its natural home.
(4) The childrens presents are under the tree.
(5) Womens sizes werent available in our citys largest store.

Exercise 23: Using quotation marks
Insert quotation marks where necessary in the following sentences.
(1) Stop that man! called the inspector.
(2) Men are made bad by bad treatment, Kelly is reported to have said.
(3) You're wrong, the minister told newsmen, if you think this is merely a publicity stunt.
(4) Men and women of Australia, he addressed the crowd, it is a crisis that we face, the people stared and listened, and only you can avert it by voting for us.
(5) This is it! I thought to myself, and jumped out of the plane. Yahoo! we all screamed as our hands linked to form a star.
(6) Early in the novel, Ged had been warned of the powers of the darkness when Ogion told him the girl herself is half witch already (p. 31).

Weaknesses in Sentence Structure

Agreement of verbs, the non-sentence and the run-on sentence are the most common structural problems for most students.

Exercise 24: Using the right tense
Verbs must agree with their subjects in *tense* and *number*. Correct the verbs used wrongly in the following sentences:
(1) 'No one,' he warned us, 'have the right to interfere in this matter.'
(2) The company have made good profits this year.
(3) Neither of the alternatives facing the council are worth considering.
(4) There was only seven officers left alive after the revolt.
(5) 'Files on Corruption' have sold well in bookstores this week.
(6) On our last camping trip we were faced with a terrible storm, our supplies were low and our boat is missing.
(7) Although he reached Moscow, Napoleon has no surrender to gloat over, no army to face, and on his return to the west, he will be caught by the bitter Russian winter.

Exercise 25: Avoiding muddled sentences

Rewrite each of the following non-sentences so that each becomes a sentence expressing a complete, unambiguous thought. Feel free to make changes, but remember to preserve the intended meaning of the original.

(1) On examining the goods they were found to be defective.
(2) Reading through the poem on a more detailed level where the images become clearer.
(3) Billy, the central character in this novel about life in a northern industrial town.
(4) Since the play is set in the present, with characters and events which are familiar to us.
(5) Rivalry between the two leaders, mutual suspicion of each other and a lack of will to cause major changes on both sides.

Exercise 26: Avoiding long sentences

Using at least two sentences in each case, rewrite each of these long sentences:

(1) Robin Hood took money from the rich and then, after keeping a nominal agent's commission, gave it to the poor and the people who received it were the poor woodcutters and the pretty widows.
(2) This novel is about the problems of prejudice and injustice that the negroes of the South had to endure and the man who suffered most was Tom because he was an innocent man who lost his life at the hands of white guards.
(3) Igor was Dracula's valet, his job was to do all the unromantic chores around the castle, his physique was very distinctive with the obligatory hump, large eyes and a disconcerting twitch at the side of the mouth.
(4) Pirates, in the main, were unlicensed raiders who could expect no help from their governments if they were caught and sometimes women pirates joined the lucrative business in the Caribbean.
(5) Mao Tse-Tung took the communists on a long walk to escape the enemy which was Chiang Kai-Shek and his men surrounded the communist base and the escape allowed Mao to establish a new base in the north.

Protecting Your Meaning

Try to be simple, clear and straightforward in your essay expression. By doing this, you will be able to hold your reader's attention and interest. Here are some hints for the protection of meaning:

Hints

1. Follow the points in your plan.
2. Deal with one thing at a time.
3. Avoid side-tracks.
4. Try not to squeeze too much into one sentence.
5. Be aware of the verbs that control each sentence.
6. Remember that words such as 'because', 'since', 'although' and 'while' must join two parts of a sentence.
7. Give each paragraph a topic sentence.
8. Check that punctuation preserves your intended meaning.
9. Avoid big, flashy words that serve no useful purpose in transmitting your meaning.
10. Re-read your essay later, as errors will stand out more clearly then.

CHAPTER 10
Formal Essay Conventions

A very formal essay would be presented as follows:

When writing essays on certain subjects, you may need to provide the reader with a synopsis, quotations, footnotes and a bibliography. This section explains those conventions and shows you how to use them.

Synopsis

A synopsis is a brief summary of the argument developed in your essay; it is not a table of contents. A synopsis would only be required in an argumentative essay. Though a synopsis may be yet another task to be performed after the essay has been completed, it is a good test of your success in developing a coherent argument. You may find examples of such summaries in magazines such as *The Bulletin*, usually in the form of an italicised paragraph under the headline of an argumentative article.

Quotations

Format of quotations

As a general rule, include short quotations of less than thirty words within the text, and use quotation marks. To represent a quotation within a quotation, use: " ' ' ". For example: Macbeth snarls "Lay on Macduff, and damned be him that first cries 'Hold, enough' " (Act V, sc. vii).

Longer quotations of more than thirty words should be set off from the text by leaving a space above and below the quotation and by indenting it a few millimetres at both margins.

Editing of quotations

To show *omissions* from quotations, use . . . (three dots; four if over a full stop). To show *additions* to the original, use [ ] square brackets. (e.g. The National Crime Authority was accused of becoming 'nothing more than an alternative [federal] police force' in the press report. A former commissioner said the NCA was not '. . . concentrating on the Mr Bigs' when he was there.)

Integrating quotations with the text of the essay

Quotations should be used to support what you have to say. In this role, a quotation should always be accompanied by your comment or observation made within the sentence. In other words, a supporting extract should not be allowed to make up a whole sentence on its own. ('Fury reddened the boy's face' (p. 214) when Mrs Mapplestead's palms, a fixture in Rob's mind, were removed.)

Acknowledging the source of quotations

For journals, newspapers, periodicals and unedited books, underline or italicise the title (e.g. The Bulletin, The Australian, Arena, Venomous Toads of Australia). For articles within a periodical or journal, or for items within an edited work, put the title in quotation marks. (e.g. 'National Affairs' in The Australian, 'The Stupefying Powers of Ordinaryman' in The Bulletin).

You should include dates of publication in footnotes and bibliographies.

Footnotes

These acknowledge and give precise reference to the source of all quotations that support what you have said in the essay. Opinions and factual material may need to be acknowledged in the same way.

Each reference is made in the form of a separate, numbered note at the bottom of each page.

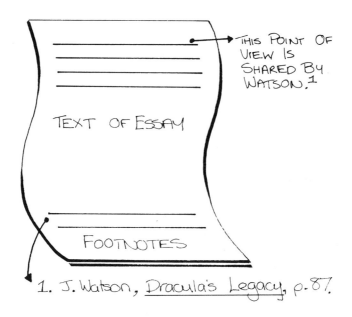

Abbreviations used in footnotes

ibid. (*ibidum*): means in the work cited immediately before

op. cit. (*opere citato*): means in the work cited before, but not the one immediately before

loc. cit. (*loco citato*): means the same page of a work cited before, but not the one immediately before passim: means 'everywhere' — the footnote refers to the entire text rather than to any one specific page

Example:
1. J. Watson, Dracula's Legacy, p. 87.   ⎤— *book by a single author*
2. S. Holmes, 'The butcher's work' in D. Serge (ed.), A Dracula Reader, p. 34.   ⎤— *item from an edited work*
3. A. Cooper, 'Transylvanian revelation' in Journal of Vampire Studies, No. 15, p. 14.   ⎤— *article from a journal*
4. ibid., p. 18.
5. Holmes, op. cit., p. 130.
6. Watson, loc. cit.
7. R. Weasle, The Dracula Legend, passim.

Bibliography

This is an alphabetical list of the sources consulted for your essay. It can refer to a book by a single author, an item from a collected or edited work or an article in a journal. It should give details of author, title, the place and date of publication, and the volume of any work in a series. Note that some editions of books are reprints; if this is the case, you must cite the year your edition was printed.

Example:
Cooper, A., 'Transylvanian revelation', Journal of Vampire Studies, No. 15, 1939.
Holmes, S., 'The butcher's work' in D. Serge (ed.), A Dracula Reader, Cooma, Spectre, 1953.
Watson, J., Dracula's Legacy, Dorrigo, Morrow and Brown, 1979.
Weasle, R., The Dracula Legend, Berridale, Strange Press, 1927.